THE

ARAMAIC
JESUS

BOOK OF DAYS

THE
ARAMAIC
JESUS
BOOK OF DAYS

40 Days of
Contemplation and Revelation

NEIL DOUGLAS-KLOTZ

This edition first published in 2025 by Hampton Roads Publishing, an imprint of Red Wheel/Weiser, LLC

With offices at:
65 Parker Street, Suite 7
Newburyport, MA 01950

Sign up for our newsletter and special offers by going to *www.redwheelweiser.com/newsletter*

Verses in the footnotes excerpted from the Holy Bible, King James Version.

Cover design by Sky Peck Design
Cover image by iStock.com
Interior by Kate Kaminski, Happenstance Type-O-Rama
Typeset in Alegreya Sans, Gill Sans, Noto Serif, and Ten Oldstyle

ISBN: 978-1-64297-059-3

Library of Congress Cataloging-in-Publication Data

Names: Douglas-Klotz, Neil, author.
Title: The Aramaic Jesus book of days : forty days of contemplation and
   revelation / Neil Douglas-Klotz.
Description: Newburyport, MA : Hampton Roads, 2025. | Includes
   bibliographical references. | Summary: "This book provides a guide to
   transformation through the way of the prophet. It offers a unique
   perspective on Jesus's teachings that addresses contemporary
   challenges, such as our relationships with nature and each other,
   and can help the reader live a more authentic, fulfilling, and
   compassionate life"-- Provided by publisher.
Identifiers: LCCN 2024034351 | ISBN 9781642970593 (trade paperback) | ISBN
   9781612834986 (ebook)
Subjects: LCSH: Jesus Christ--Words--Meditations. | Jesus
   Christ--Teachings--Meditations. | Christian life--Meditations. |
   Bible.--Criticism, interpretation, etc. | Aramaic language--Religious
   aspects--Christianity. | BISAC: RELIGION / Biblical Studies / New
   Testament / Jesus, the Gospels & Acts | BODY, MIND & SPIRIT / Healing /
   Prayer & Spiritual
Classification: LCC BT306 .D679 2025 | DDC 242/.3--dc23/eng/20241025
LC record available at https://lccn.loc.gov/2024034351

Printed in the United States of America
IBI

10 9 8 7 6 5 4 3 2 1

*For all those seekers
who are also willing to be finders.*

CONTENTS

A QUICK START GUIDE

1. **Dive in, get wet, and swim around.** To find the spiritual way of the Aramaic Jesus (Yeshua) means experiencing life from a new point of view. Don't look for a neat package of beliefs or concepts. In Yeshua's world, the human mind and heart did not function in our modern bullet points. Teachings swirled around "those with ears to hear" until absorbed, just at the right moment!

2. **You might *not* want to begin at the beginning.** Read the Introduction to receive a quick orientation and then begin using the book immediately. Eyes closed, breathe for a moment with your fingertips touching your heart and ask what you need to hear today. Then open your eyes and the book and read, as you would an oracle. Wherever you open, you will find a new message. Let your intuition guide you. Then after some days or weeks, you might feel moved to begin at the beginning for the next forty days.

3. **Meditation a day.** Each day has a short, guided contemplation that invites you to make the thought for the day into more than that—something you experience within and around you in your life, then act upon. Various themes appear and reappear, like musical motifs. They open the opportunity for light and insight to appear suddenly. Trying to figure things out tends to push such experiences away. The contemplations, which use breathing, sound, and body awareness, are essential to receiving the full benefit of what Yeshua is offering us.

4. **A forty-day retreat.** In the ancient world, forty days, about six weeks, was considered the length of time it takes to make a

breakthrough in life. If you commit a bit of time each day, you can experience miraculous results. Then, whenever your intuition taps you on the shoulder in the future, you can return to using the book as an oracle.

5. **Hunt and gather.** You can also use the appendices or index to look for particular subjects, then follow one particular thread—for instance, sayings on light. The book is meant to spark your intuition. Don't worry about doing it right or needing to know the exact pronunciation of Aramaic words. These are both well-known diversions from Yeshua's heart path.

6. **Take some time each day to release, relax, and be open to your soul's voice.** Life presents us with many seemingly urgent or serious challenges, as well as various opportunities, programs, and methods for growth. Yeshua's spiritual way shows that we need first to recalibrate our smaller self to a deeper way of breath and heart, touching our *ruha*, our soul. We can only do this with sincere heartfelt intention, together with a sense of ease and lightness.

INTRODUCTION

An Aramaic Jesus View of Life

I invite you to immerse yourself in the view of life revealed by Jesus's words through his native Aramaic language. It can literally change your life, as it did mine. What you read will be very different from what you may have heard or learned from other authorities, either religious or secular.

As I said in the "Quick Start Guide," we cannot enter Jesus's spiritual way by outlining a set of concepts or beliefs, or by giving a step-by-step program that fits everyone. Fixed concepts and beliefs form the basis of self-help programs, theologies, and academic theories. All of the latter arise long after the time of Jesus and don't apply to his way of experiencing life.

After using this book as an oracle for a bit, you can receive maximum benefit from it by following chapter-by-chapter for about six weeks. That's why this book has forty chapters. In ancient Southwest Asia (the "Middle East"), people considered forty days to be the time one needs to receive a genuine inspiration or vision, to release an entrenched memory, or to make a radical change. For instance, Moses spent forty days on the mountaintop, and Yeshua spent forty days in the wilderness following his baptism by John.

The chapters spiral though various topics, always circling around and aiming to help you deepen in Yeshua's way of perceiving life, which includes the seen and unseen worlds. Some of this may seem strange at first, since these perceptions—now labeled "mystical" or "spiritual"—are not valued in contemporary culture. Yet they were part of the human way of experiencing life for tens of thousands of years.

The Structure of the Chapters

Each chapter begins with a short reading for the day (or moment). Then you'll find a few **Key Words** that appear in Yeshua's native Aramaic language. Next, I reflect on a situation you might encounter in life and what Yeshua has to say about it in one of the four canonical Gospels or the Gospel of Thomas. His specific saying is followed by an expanded interpretation from the Aramaic text. A footnote gives the best-known translation of the same saying from the English language King James Version (KJV). The **Roots and Branches** section follows, looking briefly at the key words, roots, and their alternate meanings. Then you'll find the **Message for Today**, which invites you to consider what's going on in your life in relation to his saying. Finally, the **Contemplation** uses primarily the sensations of breathing and body awareness of the key Aramaic words; this is essential to experiencing Yeshua's more integrated, embodied view of life. Numbers in parentheses (#) refer to previous days, that is, chapters. The appendices provide references to the threads of Yeshua's prayer and Beatitudes, which can provide meditations for shorter retreats.

Please don't become sidetracked by wanting to pronounce the Aramaic exactly right. This is a common trick of our *naphsha*, the small self. First, no one knows exactly how Jesus pronounced his first-century CE Aramaic. The words in the Contemplations are key words from the Syriac Peshitta version (see the next section), and even they are pronounced differently by various Aramaic Christian groups today. I use a combination of their main pronunciations along with a nuance of the way ancient Hebrew would have been pronounced (similar to today's Samaritan language). This would have influenced native Aramaic speakers in Jesus's time.

Most important: If you feel the open sounds of the words in and around your heart, then your intention to meditate, pray, and harmonize your life will tune in your pronunciation, breathing, and inner feeling of the words to help you connect to your *ruha*-soul, using Yeshua's help. Feeling his words inside is a traditional, and effective, way to touch his atmosphere directly. If you wish later to hear and learn pronunciations for all the words in Jesus's prayer (the "Lord's Prayer") or the Beatitudes in Matthew, you can find those via audio downloads at my website. Don't skip the Contemplations. The point is not to learn ideas, but to change your way of seeing, feeling, and acting.

What's Not Here

Sources and linguistics. Yeshua's Aramaic sayings are quotes from the Syriac Aramaic version of the Gospels (the Peshitta), used by all Aramaic-speaking Christians today. This version is widely available and not a hidden source, although one needs to know how to read Semitic roots in a multileveled way (see below). Here I give only a simple parsing of the roots for all the key words. You will also not find formal scholarly transliterations (rendering into English characters with diacritical marks, like dots), but you will find them in my book *The Hidden Gospel*. If you want to find out more about the background of all this, I recommend my most recent book *Revelations of the Aramaic Jesus*, which contains a full explanation as well as an extensive bibliography of sources.

"Word-for word" Aramaic word translations. The way I interpret the sayings here is more personal than what I have done in previous books. I have offered the meanings that have helped me the most and percolated into my way of making choices in life. Ancient Semitic languages and their root-and-pattern system of meaning allow for various levels of interpretation. This means that several "literal" (word-for-word, letter-by-letter) translations can exist simultaneously.

Adding to this interweaving of meaning, ancient Semitic languages like Aramaic handle prepositions differently than we do. This is about the way people perceived time and space. The same preposition that means, for instance, "within," (*b*), also can be translated literally "among" or "around." So what appears "outside" reflects what appears "within" and vice versa. Likewise, the verbs of ancient Semitic languages (including ancient Hebrew, Canaanite, Babylonian, Egyptian, and Qur'anic Arabic) don't strictly separate past, present, and future. Linguists call these languages "synchronic," meaning that the perceptions of time we now divide can be felt as connected. Finally, there was no separation of what we call "body" and "spirit." All these factors and others that may surprise you impact how we can hear Yeshua's words.

If you are interested in the way I render the multiple meanings of the sayings here, with all the Aramaic language background, *Revelations of the Aramaic Jesus* is again your best guide. I abbreviate the *Revelations* book in notes and asides as "RAJ," *The Hidden Gospel* as "HG," and the other major source, my book *Desert Wisdom*, as "DW." You don't need to read any of these books first in order to benefit from this one. This is a book for meditation, prayer, and spiritual experience, not for textual study.

A Few Key Starters

Keeping in mind what I've said about the danger of outlining concepts, here are a few of the words essential to an ancient Semitic worldview in their Aramaic forms rendered approximately into English letters. You will encounter them frequently, and as you do, this seemingly paradoxical way of perceiving life will slowly sink in, revealing a depth you can't yet imagine.

Naphsha: The "breath" held within us for the period we live in the flesh, that is, in time and space. It creates the appearance and perception of a "personal self," an "I." I refer to it, for simplicity, as "self." The King James Version (KJV) and other versions misleadingly translate this word, or its Greek equivalent, as "life," "soul," or "self."

Ruha: The larger "breath" of Reality that holds us, including our *naphsha,* within it. It continues from before our physical birth to after our physical "death" (or "transition," a better translation from the Aramaic). I refer to it here as the "soul." The KJV translates it as "wind," "air," or "spirit." I realize that the words "self" and "soul" are used differently in various texts or psychological personality theories. (For instance, what Carl Jung refers to as the "Self" is in these terms *ruha*, the soul.)

Nuhra: Light. Not only visible light, but what awakens and illuminates all of our embodied senses—seeing, smelling, touching, hearing, tasting, and body awareness. This is not any specific perception but what sees and senses through us or within us.

Alaha: The word Yeshua uses for "God," but which would be better translated as "Reality" or "reality" (ancient Semitic languages have no capital letters). The word roots point to the union of "yes," or "something," and "no" or "nothing." It's similar to the words *Elohim* in Hebrew, *Elat* in Old Canaanite, and *Allah* in Arabic.

Malkuta: Usually translated "kingdom," but actually feminine-gendered, its roots point to an experience of both vision and the power to bring the vision into form. One of Yeshua's most used words in sayings, healing, and parables.

Leba: "Heart," the place where *naphsha* and *ruha* can come together consciously and bring "heaven to earth." Including but not limited to what we call the physical heart.

Huba: One of several different Aramaic words for "love," in this case, a consciously chosen friendship and love that can transcend or override memory as well as the seeming boundary between one life and another. The Song of Songs uses the Hebrew equivalent in the saying "love is as strong as death."

Hayye: Life and life energy, living and "livingness," across all times, before birth, during embodied life, after death.

Hakima: Sacred Sense or Holy Wisdom, that is, what unites the perceptions of all our senses within us. Feminine-gendered and better known by her later Greek name, *Sophia*.

I could expand this list, showing that the root meanings of key words in the ancient biblical and other Semitic languages, as well as the worldview and cosmology they reveal, were common to people in this region for thousands of years. As I write about in RAJ, this way of perceiving life no doubt stems from an ancient nomadic, pre-agricultural view of reality.

And a Few Key False Assumptions

In doing this work over more than four decades and reading what people say about it, particularly online, I find three major false assumptions. I address all these in more detail in *Revelations of the Aramaic Jesus*, but to save you a bit of time, they are:

1. **I am not retranslating backward from English into Aramaic.** I use as a source text the Syriac Peshitta version of the Bible (see previous discussion). The oldest copy of this version is only slightly younger than the oldest Greek version. Aramaic Christians say that they did not preserve copies of old manuscripts as something sacred, but recopied and checked them before ritually burning the old copy. They report they had scriptures in their homes for a thousand years before Western Christianity legally allowed common people to do the same.*

2. **The Syriac is a different form of Aramaic from what Jesus would have spoken.** Some ways of pronouncing the words may have been different, but *all* of the Semitic roots of the words Jesus *must have used* are the same in both first-century Palestinian Aramaic and the slightly later Syriac. Rendering the roots of ancient Semitic languages involves four things: the actual language, the worldview and way of knowing (epistemology) of these ancient peoples, one's own intention, and what one is open to experience. This is the basis of what is called in the Hebrew biblical tradition *midrash* and in the Arabic Qur'anic tradition *taw'il*. From having worked in the academic biblical

---

* See Lamsa, George. (1976). *New Testament Origin*. San Antonio: Aramaic Bible Center.

studies field for many years, I can say that virtually all scholars of biblical languages ignore the epistemology question, because a serious consideration would reveal that they are reading their own modern way of experiencing life into ancient biblical texts. This includes cultural and anthropological studies of ancient life. Simply put, human consciousness and our way of experiencing reality is not the same today as it was then.

3. **"If I only had a word-for-word translation of the Peshitta, all of Yeshua's teachings would be revealed."** I'm asked about this quite a bit. It should be clear from the previous points that this is not possible if one wishes to enter the depths of what Jesus's words and actions can reveal. Just because a person, even a native speaker, knows a form of Aramaic does not make them prepared for these depths if they don't wish to experience it. They might instead prefer to stay within a certain theological or academic conceptual framework that keeps their own life and self safely outside the frame. The same is true of the understanding of other sacred texts and languages. Just because a person knows ancient Greek, Sanskrit, Pali, Hebrew, Arabic, or Chinese, for example, does not make them "spiritual," a mystic, or even a better person. If it did, the world would be a different place. As human beings, we can make a free choice as to what we focus on in life. This is both the beauty and the terror of the way our consciousness today has evolved.

Why This Book?

This book takes an inside-out approach in relation to my previous ones on Jesus. It begins with what we may be experiencing in life, then offers us an opportunity to hear some wisdom about this from Yeshua. I have found that once people get over the shock that Jesus was talking about life in a very different way from what most branches of Christianity as well as "historical Jesus" scholars teach, their focus changes. They no longer want every phrase or saying retranslated but become passionate about applying it all to their lives. They may have spent years thinking that Jesus or their Christian upbringing was the problem and so have sought refuge in other traditions or methods, only to discover that in the end no method, path, or way is a substitute for finding one's own path.

Yeshua confirms this. He points us toward what I have called our heart's genuine "GPS" (*shrara*) as our guide through life. Awakening this deeper heart rather than its surface was one of his main messages. His words also point toward where our human consciousness is trending, and most importantly, how to work with it in a healthy way.

This book is dedicated to readers who wish to grow into their full humanity now, rediscovering how to unite inner and outer life in harmony, finding the "Cosmic Christ" within and around them. If some of us do this, it can open a new way for human beings to survive and even thrive in the future.

CHAPTER ONE

The Doorway of Anxiety

Key Words: malkuta d'Alaha, zadiquta

*When you are guided here, consider whether your situation
in life is asking you to stop, breathe, and connect with a
deeper voice within you saying: "I can!"*

Life sometimes places us in situations that prompt anxiety about the future. Comparatively, in a real emergency there is usually no time to stop and agonize; we simply act without thinking, and usually our responses are right. So how could we find a way to touch this place of direct insight more often, when we find ourselves paralyzed by expectations of the future or plagued by past memories? Yeshua counsels:

*"If you're going to be anxious and rush around about anything,
do it first with finding the 'I Can' of the cosmos within you and
how it straightens out and clarifies your life."**

Roots and Branches

The Aramaic word that Jesus must have used for "seek" (as translated in the King James version) is *buwhdayn*, meaning "to rush around, feeling hollow or empty inside." The word for "first" is *luqdam*, literally "to go back to the

---

* Matt. 6:33: "Seek ye first the kingdom of God and his righteousness, and all these things shall be added unto you."

beginning," to the *qadam* or "turning point of everything"—really our own birth as well as the birth of the universe. "Kingdom of God" (feminine gendered in Aramaic) is *malkuta d'Alaha*, so at least "queendom." Its word roots point to our soul's vision of the way ahead along with the energy to get there. This combination of vision and power resonates within us as "I can!" The word translated "righteousness" is *zadiquta*—not feeling "justified" because we hold some specific religious belief, but what clarifies and straightens out our view to see what's actually *Real*.

Message for Today

When we find ourselves trapped within a loop of worry or habitual thought, Yeshua counsels that we reconnect with the birth energy at the beginning of the cosmos. How? First, we can breathe and remember a time when we felt empowered to do something, when we felt "I can!" within us. Second, we can allow the larger "I Can" of the cosmos to flood our hearts with clarity. This is beyond our personal ego. We can then begin to experience our larger soul's voice, energy, and empowerment coming through, embracing our small self. Yeshua calls our small self the *naphsha*, the breath and sense of "I" held in these bodies for the limited time we have in the flesh. But we are really a bigger breath, a *ruha*, which is part of the "holy breath" (or "holy spirit"), containing the power and energy in nature around us. We have all experienced this empowerment, either in an emergency or when we find ourselves deeply in love. This "I can" is our soul's gift guiding us through our lives here.

Perhaps life is calling you to radically reevaluate your goals or a specific challenge facing you. The beginning of a new year or season might prompt this feeling. What do you feel compelled to do by your past actions, responsibilities accepted, or promises made to others? Are you willing to take a fresh look at all of these? To become a larger you?

CONTEMPLATION

I begin with this possibility: I am more than my body, mind, emotions, or this collection of habits. Then I interrupt all thoughts I'm having about this by breathing Yeshua's words, approximately sounded "mahl-koo-tah d'Ahl-la-ha."

Next, I breathe with these open sounds and feel them around my heart. I open to love and life energy, above, around, underneath, and within me, using a feeling connection to Yeshua to help me. This is the doorway to *malkuta*. I settle in this easy, natural breath and feeling.

When I feel more neutral about the life situation I face, I breathe the word sounded "zah-dee-qoo-tah," clear and straight perception. It resonates from the heart ("zah") to the middle of my forehead ("dee"), down to the belly ("qu"), then back to the heart ("tah"). I use this opportunity to see, sense, and feel clearly what is before me.

When I feel ready, I open my eyes and go about my day, facing what life brings me as best I can each moment. When tempted to forget and return to an old pattern, I again feel myself surrounded by *malkuta*, a sphere of love and empowerment always present. I have the courage to follow this feeling and embrace the energy that comes with it.

CHAPTER TWO

Your Real Home

Key Words: tubwayhun, b'rukh

*When you are guided here, or when you feel abandoned, take
the opportunity to remember that the breath rising and falling
in your body is a gift: the first thing to enter, the last to leave.
Your personal breath is the doorway to your real home.*

Like you, I have faced personal or family emergencies and found I needed
to catch my breath, to focus completely on the air slowly going in and out
of my lungs. It's certainly one way to dull physical pain. But there's much
more to it, according to Yeshua. In Aramaic, the same word, *ruha*, can
mean "breath," "spirit," "air," "wind," or the "soul" itself—that is, the part of
us always connected to the Big Breath, the source of life. In the beginning
of the Beatitudes in Matthew, Yeshua counsels:

> "Blessedly ripe, in the right moment, are those who rest in ruha as
> their first and last possession, their real home. To them is coming—
> at the same moment—the light and empowerment streaming
> through nature and the cosmos."*

Roots and Branches

We have seen *malkuta* (usually mistranslated "kingdom") just before
this (1), the "I Can" of Reality. "Of heaven" is *d'shmaya*, which means

---

* Matt. 5:3: "Blessed are the poor in spirit, for theirs is the kingdom of heaven."

that this "I Can" produces waves of light and sound that extend without limit around us, in time and space. "Poor in spirit" is *l'meskenae b'rukh*. We are literally both "within" and "among" (*b*) the soul's breath (*rukh*). We are not "poor" but rather tethered (*mesken*) to the honest realization that our only possession in life is our breathing, which is itself owned by the Big Breath, which Yeshua calls *ruha d'qudsha* ("the sacred or holy breath"). At any time, we then can experience being in a joyfully ripe—in the *now*—moment: the Aramaic *tubwayhun* (usually translated "blessed").

Message for Today

The most joyous, appropriate state we can experience, says Yeshua, is to be at one with the One (*Alaha*) in this moment. He asks us to regard any and every breath as a doorway to a greater sense of empowerment—*malkuta*—if we are willing to rest in our own personal powerlessness and connect first with the Big Breath.

This concept may be hard to imagine, but actually we do it all the time—while we sleep or dream. Our personal breath connects to a larger one, which is only love, life energy, and light. Our body continues to breathe without our conscious attention, and sometimes real visions and healing come in sleep if we are ready. "Do I have the courage to let go and trust that this larger breath will breathe me?"

Perhaps life is calling you to not only "catch your breath," but rest within the larger breath that streams life and love from above, around, underneath, and within you. I frequently ask myself: "Can I take this leap and feel that my breath is part of the Holy Breath/Spirit?"

CONTEMPLATION

Before going to sleep at night, I rest my forehead on the earth or floor, or imagine in my body awareness that I am doing so while I'm lying in bed. I release everything that has happened during the day that I don't need to keep around for tomorrow. I don't dwell on individual impressions.

Then I rise (or imagine I'd doing so) and feel my breath in or around the heart. I feel the awareness of it opening above me, way beyond my room and building. I connect there with a bigger breath of love, thankfulness, and life energy and allow it to stream down through me like liquid light—through my eyes, ears, head, throat, heart, belly, hips, legs, and feet, down into the earth underneath me, even to the center of the earth. There I feel another source of warm love and life, the heart of Holy Wisdom, reflecting back up through me.

Breathing in feeling the word "tooh-bway-hoon" and out the word "b'rookh," I feel this stream of love coming from both above and beneath me into the heart. Then, as I breathe out, it flows through my heart into the space around me. If I am still awake, I rest in the doorway of this Big Breath, my real home, and enter it.

CHAPTER THREE

The Greatest Gift
to a Friend

Key Words: huba d'rab

*When you are guided here, or are wondering how much concern
to feel for a family member, friend, or lover, take the opportunity
to allow yourself to be flooded only with thankfulness that you've
been given this opportunity to care.*

We live at a time when no one wants to be considered codependent, and
everyone wants everyone else to be free to live their own lives. At the
same time, our natural self, resting in the breath, feels a connection with
a family member, friend, or lover. Being related to others is a large part
of what makes us human beings. We are warned by therapists about
"smother love," but the type of emotive love they talk about is one that
concerns itself with the questions: "How will this action make *me* look?"
"Will it make *me* feel good, bad, or (even more subtly) guilt-free?" This
so-called love is ultimately all about the small self, the *naphsha*. Yeshua
offers the following advice:

> *"The most essential, creative, nurturing love is the one when you
> temporarily lay aside your preference for your small self and
> treat that of your soul-friend or lover as equal to your own."**

---

* John 15:13: "Greater love hath no man than this, that a man lay down his life
for his friends."

Roots and Branches

Yeshua uses the phrase *huba d'rab* for what the KJV translates as "greater love." *Huba* is the type of love that grows slowly from tolerance to respect to friendship to something that, according to the Hebrew equivalent used in the Song of Songs, is "as strong as death." What the KJV renders confusingly here as "life" is really *naphsha*, our usual preference for our own small self—its life, health, and concerns. This preference is healthy within limits; we only lay it aside in special cases. According to Yeshua, such a special case occurs when we have a deep relationship with a friend or lover, a *rahmawhy*, based on a different Aramaic word for love—the type that streams through us as an act of creation, like a mother giving birth from her womb (13), *rahm*, from the same Semitic root.

Message for Today

Too often I've heard this saying interpreted, as have many others in the Gospels, to mean "if you sacrifice yourself now, you will get your reward later." While life during the time we have a *naphsha* is not always easy, the only value in sacrificing our *naphsha* is when we aren't aware of it at all, not when said sacrifice is requested or commanded by someone else or by some institution. We can all remember a time when we simply forgot ourselves in love. What was happening? Probably we were overcome by thankfulness and an almost miraculous sense of joy streaming through us. The small self disappeared, even for a moment, from the force of a more powerful, nurturing (*rab*) love, not from a sense of duty, shame, or guilt.

Perhaps life is calling you to consider what to feel or do about the suffering or predicament of someone you're close to. The first step may be to simply feel grateful that you have such a deep heart connection. Then step away from all concerns about what you should do. Instead, bring in more love and thankfulness from the greater Source that is above, underneath, and around you—not enclosed within the walls of your skin. This love breaks through restrictions and boundaries; it offers a new birth to another—and to yourself at the same time.

CONTEMPLATION

I place my forehead on the floor or earth or imagine myself doing so. As before, I breathe out, feeling my heart above my head, which rests and releases all tension in my forehead, neck, and shoulders. Then I rise up again as I breathe feeling Yeshua's words, approximately sounded "hooba d'rahb." What could be easier, what could be lighter in the heart when I clear space on its surface from any concern for myself? Perhaps two or three more rounds of bowing and rising up again clear my heart even more. I visualize the other person along with myself within the light of thankfulness and the greater love. Does any outward action appear? If not, I leave it be for now. Perhaps there is nothing to be done outwardly.

Laying the small self aside takes practice. Don't be discouraged if it immediately pops up again, demanding attention. Simply add more love, more thankfulness, more *huba d'rab*. Eventually, the *naphsha* learns to return to this feeling more often, even after it forgets.

CHAPTER FOUR

Fresh Food Delivered from Soul to Self

Key Words: bar nasha, leba

When you are guided to this day, enjoy the opportunity to expand your horizons about how food appears in your life.

Perhaps no other subject takes up as much space online as that of food and diet: What's better for our health, what is more "natural," which foods are better for the planet and the climate? You will find endless debates about this, in which people can become very heated. Yeshua comments:

"Not what goes into a limited self's mouth perverts them, circling them back toward the small self, but what comes out of the mouth. . . . What goes into the mouth passes into the belly and then out. What goes out of the mouth proceeds from a person's heart, the center of their attention and action, creating their world. This can isolate them in their small self, veiling them."*

---

* Matt. 15:11, 17, 18: "Not that which goeth into the mouth defileth a man, but that which cometh out of the mouth, this defileth a man. Whatever entereth in at the mouth goeth into the belly, and is cast out into the draught. But those things which proceed out of the mouth come forth from the heart; and they defile the man."

Roots and Branches

What the KJV translates here as "man" is the Aramaic *bar nasha,* any child of humanity, viewed as a self that is limited in flesh for a certain time and space. The word usually translated "defile" is the Aramaic *msayeb,* something that encloses the self, causing it to circle back on itself and ultimately separates a person from *ruha,* the always-on breath that connects us to all other human beings. Heart is *leba* in Aramaic, the center of love, courage, and will. It's the doorway through which our soul-*ruha* can feed our self-*naphsha* whatever is necessary for our life here.

Message for Today

Yeshua would like us to open our limited self to our unlimited soul, using our heart's ability to freely choose at any moment. We live here in limited bodies, which have their own rhythms, so we tend to become creatures of rhythm—that is, habit. Some of these are good, but not all. Yet our flesh is always changing, even down to the cells of our body changing completely over a period of seven to ten years. Taken on the simplest level, can we sense the food our soul wants us to eat now rather than what we ate ten years ago?

On another level, our *ruha*-soul is not ours alone, but connected with that of every other person, as one. As human consciousness has become more self-focused and selfish, Yeshua enjoins us to make choices not only for our own self, but for the self of all humanity and all selves, including nature. In past ages, our self was mostly tribal; the way of human beings in the future must change. As he says in his prayer, "set us free from *bisha*" (Matt. 6:13, KJV: ". . . deliver us from evil," 27).

Perhaps life is calling you to open to your soul-force, not only in spiritual things, but even down to matters of flesh and body. In the Gospel of Thomas, Yeshua's students ask him, "What diet should we observe?" Yeshua answers, "Don't lie and don't do what you hate, because everything is uncovered within the connected light and sound that spreads through time and space—heaven." His simple diet might be: connect to the soul, then hear, see, and sense what food it wants to offer the small self.

CONTEMPLATION

When I contemplate a close-to-the-bone issue like food, I touch upon a remembrance of my limited time in a body. I want to maintain this gift of life so that I can fulfill whatever I came into flesh to learn, love, and realize.

So I breathe the words "bar nah-sha" in my heart—the light-filled enclosure that allows what is temporary and limited in me (*nasha*) to radiate (*bar*) the timeless and unlimited. When I bring the question of physical food into the mirror of my heart, can I keep opening my heart (now breathing "leb-ah") and start clearing the veils of memory, thought, and emotion that cloud the surface of the heart and obstruct my *ruha*'s radiance? It's waiting to shine all the way into my flesh. What is truly ripe for me right now?

CHAPTER FIVE

Heart of Possibility

Key Words: abwun d'bashmaya

When you are guided to this day, take the opportunity to visualize and sense a larger life unfolding around you.

In pursuing any goal, we are often advised, "begin at the beginning." But where *is* the real beginning? From Yeshua's point of view, any real beginning is part of the Beginning that continues to radiate and unfold from the first spark of the cosmos. Each of us, both individually and collectively, unfolds a world through our shared human *ruha's* consciousness. Although perhaps difficult for us to understand today, Aramaic and the other ancient Semitic languages base themselves on verbs rather than nouns, on processes rather than separate subjects and objects (either material or mental) residing in some fixed "space." To *live* in ancient Hebrew or Aramaic was the first sound, the first verb, the first breath, the original meditation. Yeshua begins his well-known prayer like this:

Creating, parenting, birthing Breath coming into form now.
Spreading, shining, radiating through all waves of sound and light,
heard or unheard by human ears,
seen or unseen by human eyes,
named or unnamed by human lips.*

---

* Matt. 6:9: "Our Father which art in heaven." See RAJ for more on the gender issues in Jesus's words.

Roots and Branches

What the KJV translates as "father" is *abwun*, a derivative of father but expanding into all parenting (ABw), beyond contemporary fixed ideas of gender, through sound and breath (U) into a middle space between self and soul, *naphsha* and *ruha*. This middle space ("oo") can be felt in the human heart (which is where the sound "abwoon" resonates), reminding us of how the mystery of life comes into each form (N) each moment, including what we call ourselves. This living, creating process is always going on throughout the universes, seen and unseen. The way this all appears in our time and space is via vibration and light unfolding without any seeming limit, *shemaya*. Just so we don't become too satisfied with our own explanations, the two sounds prefacing *shemaya* are *d* and *b*, both prepositions, which show us that *abwun's* creative process can be sensed emanating from, as well as along with and within, this universe of sound and light. The sound and light that we perceive create what we call time (unfolding in duration) and space (unfolding in extent).

Message for Today

Devotion is a miraculous feeling, opening the heart to something or someone that causes us to feel awe, thankfulness, and love. If we hold rigidly onto any particular picture or ideal of that beloved, however, the process of grasping tends to circle the feeling back to ourselves, trapping us in our own prison of mere belief, thought, or emotion.

The Aramaic words remind us that we need to hold *any* ideal of Reality or divinity very lightly; otherwise, the light and breath of the *ruha*-soul cannot penetrate from the unseen through our heart's self-imposed veils. So a beginning like *abwun d'bashmaya*—really all verb, no subject or object—invites us to breathe with as much love and awe as we can. To then resonate, open, release, and bring in more love. We can use words like this to help center our heart's awareness. Or simply breathe and feel where they lead us. While in the flesh we have the gift of choice, so throughout his teaching, Yeshua recommends that we use this gift wisely.

CONTEMPLATION

Breathing "ah-bwoo-n," I feel the sounds in or near my heart area. Then I intone the word softly, feeling my heart resonating. After I finish judging or admiring my own voice (a common occurrence), I gradually let go of any feeling that I am doing anything. Repeated over time the prayer or practice begins to do me, instead of me doing it.

I open to see, hear, sense, and feel a wider world of possibility around me. How am I not seeing or feeling clearly? What am I really looking for? What would life be like if I knew? Over time and with repetition, my sense of where "I" am interweaves with a wider cosmos of light, name, and sound. Breathing "d'bahsh-may-ah," I am welcomed to my new, wider home.

After spending some time with this contemplation, I restart my day or whatever I'm doing, trusting that the wordless feeling conveyed through the prayer will continue to work within me.

CHAPTER SIX

What Could Be More Spacious?

Key Words: nethqadash shmakh

When you are drawn or guided to this day, embrace the opportunity to feel where in your heart you could feel more ease and openness.

I often hear that someone wants to follow their heart rather than their mind. Yet in Yeshua's time, there was only a word for heart, not mind. So when the surface of the heart becomes veiled or clogged up with unhelpful self-images, emotions, or memories of the past, the heart cannot feel or see clearly. As human consciousness developed over the past few thousand years, you could say that "mind" gradually separated from "heart." Over the same time, the collective human *naphsha* also gradually separated from nature. This made it increasingly difficult to feel part of either one humanity or nature. That's where we are today. As a first step, perhaps if we paid more attention to the clarity of our hearts rather than simply wanting to feel emotion—any emotion—we might be able to dispense with the idea of a separate mind and the alienation it entails. As a prelude to his prayer, Yeshua reminds his listeners that:

> *"The Breathing Life of All, Abwun, holds in its hand knowingly whatever you are anxious and boiling over about, even before you ask. . . ."**

---

* Matt. 6:8: "your Father knoweth what things ye have need of, before ye ask him."

So first, we can deal with our heart's boiling-over anxiousness (1). After the prayer's opening words praising the heart of possibility (5), Yeshua recommends that we release the build-up of impressions on our hearts to better sense a connection of light with our soul:

> *Clear out heart space for the name-light-vibration of Abwun to focus our lives.*[†]

Roots and Branches

Another of the "mother" root sounds uniting ancient Hebrew, Aramaic, and Arabic is QDSh, *qadash* in Aramaic ("hallowed" in the KJV). This shows an open space ready to be filled with whatever is necessary for the moment. What Reality holds in its hand is what the heart really wants. The word translated "need" is a form of *metbᶜa,* also meaning anxiousness or boiling-over impatience (1). Yeshua's antidote for our personal anxiety and collective heart-blindness is to clean house in our hearts so that the "name" (*shem*) of Reality can move in. This is not necessarily a specific name in words, but from its roots (ShM), the atmosphere, light, and presence of the larger Reality, *Alaha.*

Message for Today

Thousands of years ago, the human *naphsha* was less individuated, both more tribal and communal, which didn't necessarily mean we were more wise. Witness all of the destruction by ancient civilizations described by the Bible. Just as today, whole cultures could become rotten (*bisha*), and Yeshua foresaw the potential for the entire prophetic tradition of Abraham, Sarah, and Hagar to go in this direction. Hence, he not only comforted the poor but disrupted religious and political authority.

Ultimately, we need to take care of our own heart first, then allow whatever clarity arises to offer us a fresh view of what is truly ours to do. Perhaps life is calling you now to allow more spaciousness into the

---

† Matt. 6:9: "Hallowed be thy name."

feeling of your heart. This can also mean taking time out from running around searching for what you believe you need, either outwardly or inwardly.

CONTEMPLATION

In many sayings and stories, Yeshua invites us to take a sabbath moment. I don't need to wait for a particular holy day or season to do this. As I breathe the words "neth-qah-dahsh shem-ahkh," creating spaciousness for light, I can enter a "sabbath breath" anytime.

As I feel my breathing in or around the heart, I place one hand lightly over the middle of my chest and allow my body awareness to settle there. Heartbeat, breathing, spaciousness. More ease, more openness. I can relax and let go, centered there, without the surface of the heart babbling with automatic, habitual thinking or emotion.

If you feel a special relationship to this line of Yeshua's prayer, as I do, bring the sounds of these words into your heart. Connecting through him can help focus the light within you, his heart-power strengthening your own. I use his *shem*-atmosphere to help me clear space in my heart until I can once again make my own direct connection to Abwun.

CHAPTER SEVEN

A Bigger Heart-Power

Key Words: nehwey sabyanach

When you are guided to this day, take the opportunity to receive the gift of your heart's inborn power to choose. It's already yours, waiting to be discovered, much stronger than you think.

Sometimes what we need is not more information, more resources, more learning, or even more effort, but rather a bigger power of heart and desire. The courage to choose. Fortunately, from Yeshua's point of view, this larger power is already ours and can accomplish anything. In the fourth line of his prayer, he says:

"Let the Breath of life create a new appearance of heart-desire in and through me, uniting heaven and earth, everywhen and here-now in my life."*

Roots and Branches

The Aramaic word *nehwey* begins this phrase in Yeshua's prayer, which most translations ignore or only translate as "done." Its roots (NHW) reveal that a larger breath of life, the Big Breath (HW), is creating a new appearance (N) of what follows next, in this case, a Big Heart

---

* Matt. 6:10: "Thy will be done on earth, as *it is* in heaven."

power (*sabyanach*, "will" in the KJV). This power of *saba*, which Yeshua also mentions when he performs healings, unites opposites in us. Here he mentions "heaven" (*shemaya*) and "earth" (*ar`ah*), but these stand for all "twos" that emerge from Reality in our human consciousness when we are born into time and space. *Shemaya* and *ar`ah* include wave and particle, community and individuality, timelessness and limited time, space without boundary and the point of *here*.

Message for Today

Forty-plus years ago, when I first began to explore Yeshua's Aramaic words, I felt completely out of my depth. I didn't know where or how to begin. Yet whenever I was tempted to give up, my heart opened with a larger power, one I knew could not be my own. Sitting on a hillside in a forest in northern California, I had the clear image of water emerging from a spring at the top of a mountain, then flowing and gathering into a large stream as it rushed downhill. As I began to learn to pray the prayer in Aramaic, I was continually led to a person who could help me, or I would enter a bookstore I had never visited in a strange city and was led to a book I needed. In short, I know this prayer—and specifically this line—can work miracles.

Perhaps you feel called to let go of all of your excuses not to take a step in what you feel is an impossible (or at least improbable) direction. Feelings of insecurity or inadequacy can often paralyze us. Yet these emotions are all based on memory—the past, including the past experiences of others who tell you what *they* think is possible. Is there a deeper passion welling up from within you that leads you beyond your small self and allows the gift of a Big Heart to activate your life? Contrary to what you may have been told, such inspiration is not something reserved for special people. It is available to every human being as our soul's gift.

CONTEMPLATION

Readers of my other books or visitors to my website may already know or have learned the whole fourth line of this prayer from the audio and video freely available there: *nehwe sabyanach aykana d'bashmaya aph b'ar`ah*. But don't wait to learn the whole line, start now. The Big Heart is available to anyone, no matter what language they speak.

I breathe in feeling "neh-way" and out feeling "sahb-yan-ach," using the sounds to tune myself to the person who said them. Help is here: I can feel Yeshua speaking these words in the deepest part of my heart. As he says to his students in the Gospel of John just before he leaves them: "I in you, you in me." I piggyback on his trust, his confidence in the larger Reality of Alaha. For at least a moment, I forget my *naphsha*. Then as I continue to breathe, I find my *naphsha* in the Big Breath, my heart within the Big Heart of the cosmos.

CHAPTER EIGHT

Enlightenment and Endarkenment: Conjoined Twins

Key Words: nuhra, heshukha, nuhra d'shrara

When you are guided or mysteriously drawn to this day, feel your heart capable of containing all that you believe you know and all that you believe you don't know. Then live between.

What we regard as a fact is based on what we think we can know or find out about our outer perception of reality. When we broaden our view and begin to question the basis of our measurements of both time and space, we edge toward the ultimate question: "How do we know anything?" That is, what is consciousness?

For Yeshua and the prophets before him, there was a larger Knower, which people called by various names, sometimes translated as "god" or "goddess." Yeshua taught that the human being itself was not a fixed body but more like a conversation convened by Holy Wisdom (*Hakima* in Aramaic), a conversation between knowing and unknowing. This created what we now call consciousness. What we perceive as light and darkness arises within this field of *Hakima*, or translated differently, Sacred Sense. What arises as a unity from this field is our perception of our "I," connected to the source of that "I," *Alaha*. When we dive into our heart's depths, it clarifies and directs us toward what we need to know and do. The cosmological hymn in John 1 expresses this inner reality of the true, connected "I" as embodied in Yeshua, awaiting to be awakened in every human being:

> *"Within the whole living conversation of Reality arises the life energy and light, the consciousness, of human beings. Insight, light, and knowing appear along with ignorance, darkness, and unknowing. And darkness does not tread upon, stamp out, or overtake the light. . . . This light of right direction is kindled in every human being coming into time and space."**

Roots and Branches

Earlier in this passage (John 1:1), the "Word" at the beginning is *melta*, also meaning a conversation, a clear reference to late biblical mentions of Holy Wisdom (for instance, in Sirach). "Life" is *hayye*, life energy. "Men" is always *nasha*, any human being (4). "Light" and "shineth" are both forms of *nuhra*, which is not only light perceived by the eyes, but also all ways of knowing and experiencing, through the heart and "mind." Likewise, "darkness" is *heshukha*—unknowing, "inexperiencable." What is usually translated "comprehend" (a form of *drekh*) also means to tread upon, stamp out, or overtake (as in a race). The "true light" is *nuhra d'shrara*, the clarity that shows us the right direction: the "GPS" found in every heart.

Message for Today

Hakima, Sacred Sense, gathers our sense impressions every moment. Without this happening, nothing could either "make sense" or remain

---

* John 1:4, 5, 9: "In him was life; and the life was the light of men. And the light shineth in the darkness; and the darkness comprehended it not. . . . That was the true light, which lighteth every man that cometh into the world." For a more complete discussion of this, see *RAJ*, chapter 7.

"obscure" (a word originally meaning "endarkened"). To receive real insight, rather than just repeat or rehearse memories from our past, we need to break out of the prison of our small self, by finding the middle of light and dark, the true knowing of the deep heart. Perhaps our present experiences are calling us to do this right now.

CONTEMPLATION

I breathe an easy, natural breath in or around my heart, first feeling "nooh-rah," light—my past perception of my life and my self, everything I believe to be certain or fixed. Then I breathe the word "hay-shuk-ha," the larger field of unknowingness and mystery. None of what I formerly believed may be true now. Even less matters for my next breath. Holding the limited light of memory and the darkness of unknowing together, can I allow my heart to contain them both, allowing one to cancel out the other?

This can feel like jumping off a cliff. But as the hymn in John 1 continues, when everything—all the temporary light and darkness—cancels itself out, then what remains is the *nuhra d'shrara*, the light of clear direction, waiting to radiate through me. It already creates my sense of self and my perception of the world, from the beginning of life until now. I breathe "noor-rah d'shrara," clarity for *now*—not yesterday, or the days, decades, and millennia before.

Cultivate a bit of patience with this contemplation. The unraveling may take several tries before the light before you were born brings you back to your soul's eye view: like the one you had as a newborn infant.

CHAPTER NINE

Simply Less Self

Key Words: meskina . . . malkuta d'alaha

When you are guided to this day, accept the gift of forgetting your naphsha, its concerns and activities, just for a moment.

We live in an era when self-assertion, self-affirmation, self-worth, self-help (and in general all "selfness") are valued as the highest good. There are, of course, times when one needs to strengthen one's sense of inner integrity or honesty. But at other times, an overconcern with our individual self—with doing more and accomplishing more—can lead us to burn out, either physically or emotionally.

Yeshua's Beatitudes in Matthew offer a depth process that begins with finding our home in the breath (2). He uses a slightly different form of the "blessed ripeness" word in Luke, *tubwaykhun* ("ripe are *you*,") intending it as a wake-up call for those who are already thinking too much of themselves. He was, after all, surrounded by religious officials and their hangers-on who believed themselves superior to those who were supposed to be in their care.

We don't, however, need to cast all blame on spiritual authorities (ancient or contemporary) who without any realization themselves don't use the keys they have and don't permit others to do so (see Luke 11:52 and Gospel of Thomas Saying 39).* We all sometimes need to get

---

* Thomas 39: "The Pharisees and the scholars have taken the keys of knowledge and have hidden them. They have not entered, nor have they allowed those who want to enter to do so."

the message: "Just stop! It's not all about you." Likewise Yeshua warns his students:

> "Ripe are you when you realize there is nothing for you to hold onto. Then the vision and empowerment of Reality can begin to take hold of you."†

Roots and Branches

The word usually translated "poor" is the Aramaic *meskina*, best rendered as "just holding on." In the parallel saying in Matthew, Yeshua points his listeners to their breathing and its connection to the Big Breath (2). Here it's more simple: *nothing* to hold onto—your self, any idea, or anything you can perceive in material reality. His message: less self means more soul, less *naphsha* naturally leads to more *ruha*. Clear out the inner clutter and allow your heart to reveal your "thinner" self, the one transparent enough to let the light of Reality shine through.

Message for Today

One could easily say that the world today simply has too much *doing* in general (for instance, economies that don't grow are "unhealthy"), and that even attempts to "fix" things often bring more negative unintended consequences. While we may not all return to a shared sabbath day, might it be possible to return to regular retreat, a year of reduced activity, or a sabbath moment every day? Do we really always need to see ourselves doing something "worthy," or is that just another selfie ego-trap? Only you can answer this question, which is why Yeshua frames these Beatitudes using the direct form *tubwaykhun*: "Ripe are *you* when . . ."

Perhaps life is calling you to Yeshua's tonic, which may feel initially like poison to your sense of who you think you are. Can you trust that if you just stop for a moment, or a day, your *ruha*-soul will renew you?

---

† Luke 6:20: "Blessed be ye poor: for yours is the kingdom of God."

"Won't the world fall apart?" To stop thinking about one's self may take a bit of practice, unless you're in a state of love, devotion, or thankfulness. These are best pre-tonics I have found.

CONTEMPLATION

I begin by feeling my heart as a lens, using Yeshua's word "meskeena" to help me clear out some of the impressions, memories, thoughts, and emotions preventing my *ruha*'s light from streaming through. I find that connecting to Yeshua even through this one small word can help divert my attention from myself. I can then return to the breath, word, and feeling of clearing many times throughout my day. It's always there in the background, waiting for me to let go enough in the moment so that the larger "I Can" of Reality, *malkuta d'Alaha*, can break through. I invite Reality's empowerment to show me my next step in life.

CHAPTER TEN

Who Is Saying "I Can't"?

Key Words: teyte malkutakh

When you are drawn or guided to this day, take the opportunity to ask yourself this question. Then recalibrate to the big "I Can" streaming from the Heart of Possibility, Abwun, into your heart. Use the fuel of unhelpful memories to burn what stands in your way.

When confronted with a seemingly impossible situation or unresolvable conundrum, I have often returned to this line of Yeshua's prayer, as well as the one before it (6). Sometimes the reason for a lack of "self-confidence" is that my *naphsha*-self really needs to stop and recalibrate with my soul, *ruha*. Often this recalibration not only resolves my anxiety but also releases and transforms memories of the past or past voices who, perhaps with good intentions, told me that "I can't." Yeshua counsels that, just as we can allow Reality's light-life energy-love (*shem*) to clear our heart, we can also allow it to say "I can" in the voice of our soul, the always-on Big Breath. From clearing heart-space, his prayer continues in line three:

Abwun—let arrive, with urgency, your voice of vision and power, your I Can, here and now!*

---

* Matt. 6:10: "Thy kingdom come."

Roots and Branches

The word usually translated "your kingdom" is the Aramaic *malkutakh* (1), gendered feminine (as is its equivalent used in the Greek version of the Gospels, *basileia*). The roots MLKU show a process continuing from a beginning to its natural ending (ML) energized by a fiery power (KU), like the growth of nature in springtime. The ancients saw fire as a living being, as they did all of nature's elements. The fire consumed what was past, dry enough to burn. It could both purify the earth as well as provide warmth and heat. The word usually translated "come" is the Aramaic *teytey*, literally "come-come"—meaning come *now*!

Message for Today

What do we do with all of the extra stuff that clouds our heart, paralyzing our ability to act ripely? According to Yeshua's prayer, we burn it. We burn all past memories that no longer serve us in order to power up the vision of *now*, which our soul is streaming to us, trying to reach us through the static. We burn away the static by thinning out the unnecessary firewalls we have placed around our heart through being mesmerized by popular culture, which relentlessly intones that only outer, measurable reality exists.

Perhaps life is calling you to a larger vision, one that not only stretches your small sense of self but shatters it altogether. Scary? Yes, but we can prepare for this process by willingly placing our *naphsha* in a bonfire of *malkuta*. Big Love with Vision resurrects a newly reborn *naphsha*, like a phoenix rising. Our small self exists as long as we live in time and space, but we can free our hearts in the present and prepare for our journey beyond physical death, when that self gets thinned anyway. Why not, as they say, "get ahead of the game"?

CONTEMPLATION

I center breathing in and around the heart, beginning with a few breaths clearing space in the heart's mirror (6). Then I bring in what I can muster of sincere, heartfelt intention to say, in my own words: "Bring it on now, I'm ready!" Or in Aramaic "tay-tay mahl-koo-takh." I feel breath, heartbeat, and intention meshing with the words. After frequent repetition with feeling, these words, connecting me to Yeshua, become touchstones that appear in my heart whenever I need them.

To complete, I slowly open my eyes and notice the wordless feeling. I stand up and begin to walk in a rhythm of four with the inner sound—mal-koo-takh-(rest)—breathing with energy. I use the words to center my body awareness in the heart. My soul says, "I can!"

CHAPTER ELEVEN

Even More Soul Food

Key Words: habwlan lachma

*When you are guided to this day, it could be time to consider
all the sources of sustenance that appear in your life each day.*

Although it has become a cliché to talk about food for the soul, from Yeshua's viewpoint all of our food actually comes from the soul-*ruha*. Contrary to what we may have heard, it is our soul that saves us rather than we needing to save it. There is no boundary, no fixed border, between the soul—our always-on breath of life, love, and energy—and our individual self-*naphsha*, the limited breath held in this flesh for a period of time.

Likewise, for Yeshua there is no separation between the food we eat to feed our bodies, and the sustenance we receive as wisdom, inspiration, emotional support, or enlightening ideas, which can all reroute us onto the track of our soul's path. All these are included in his word for "bread," *lachma*. So his prayer recommends we ask through our heart for Reality to shape things this way:

> *"Create for us the lachma we need for each and every moment of
> light that we have in this embodied life."**

---

* Matt. 6:11: "Give us this day our daily bread."

Roots and Branches

The word translated "give us" (*habwlan*) is not a demand. It is an acknowledgment that everything is created and formed in the larger reality of *Abwun*, the constantly creating Reality, the root of which we find within the word. So we are simply, willingly, aligning our selves with this ongoing flow of creating. The word translated "day" is *yauma*, based on the Aramaic and Hebrew word for an embodied "drop" of a light-wave, a day. In this sense a "day" could last any number of years as humanity measures them today (which is what the Psalmist says, 90:4). The word usually rendered "daily" (or "for our needs") is *d'sunqanan*, which points to an enclosed circle of what is needed *now*, rather than what was needed in the past or could be needed in the future.

Message for Today

Yes, this well-known line of Yeshua's prayer does counsel us against any sort of hoarding. Wealth, wisdom, intellectual knowledge, and emotional resilience are gifted to us and created through us in order to be shared, just as is physical food. But at the same time, we are reminded not to limit our expectations: what may have been needed or seemed possible at one moment does not limit what we can receive in the next. Some effort on the part of our small self may be required, but the limitless creativity of the soul is always on call, if we don't block its activity.

Perhaps life is calling us to first acknowledge everything we receive each day in terms of this wider view of food. And instead of demanding anything, to immerse ourselves in thankfulness and love. This opens the doorway to receiving what "I" need for *this illuminated moment*.

CONTEMPLATION

Breathing in "hahb-lahn" and out "lach-mah," sensing the heart, I feel the center of my chest open in thanks and love. I take some time to do this and don't proceed further until I can feel myself surrounded by the soul's nurturing presence. I am not presenting the divine with a list of demands but acknowledging, with love and respect, the source from which everything arises. A larger Reality surrounds me, one that is underneath, around, and beyond the appearances of what I perceive on the outside.

When I'm able to drop into this soul-space, I leave room in my heart for the soul's inspiration about whatever challenge or need life is putting on my plate right now.

I continue breathing the phrase as I open my eyes. I remember it as much as possible as I go about my day and notice where new opportunities for sustenance and nurturance appear.

CHAPTER TWELVE

The Real Source of Hunger and Thirst

Key Word: khenuta

When you are drawn to this day, accept the opportunity to dedicate yourself to inner honesty and outer justice. Practice refusing to lie to yourself.

There comes a time in life when the "white lies" we tell ourselves need to end. Perhaps we needed them when we were younger, simply to survive. I'm not talking about seemingly impossible past goals. As we have seen in Yeshua's teachings, many things can be possible and real if we have the clarity of heart to see the necessary steps to them. I'm referring here to inflated views of our self, status, and entitlement, against which Yeshua repeatedly warns us in Luke's Beatitudes (9, 29).

In the fourth Beatitude in Matthew, he points to a tough honesty with ourselves that at the same time affects our dealings with others:

> *"In happy ripeness are those who discover their real hunger and thirst—a life in which they are honest with themselves and deal justly with others. If they are hungry and thirsty enough, such a life is created around them."**

---

* Matt. 5:6: "Blessed are they which do hunger and thirst after righteousness: for they shall be filled."

Roots and Branches

The key word here, usually translated abstractly as "righteousness," is *khenuta*, an Aramaic word that brings together inner honesty and outer justice. This unity can only live in a heart, *leba*, which is free of the self-hypnosis of self-delusion. The word translated "filled" is *nesbuwn*, from *saba* (root SB), a new outer reality created through the heart's desire of the cosmos acting through us (5).

Message for Today

Emergencies, or the push and pull of immediate need, often reveal to us what feels clearly as a more real life. For a largely impoverished and traumatized audience, well accustomed to actual hunger and thirst, Yeshua's words were even more powerful than they may sound to most of us today. To feel this need is one of the reasons that many people now subconsciously undertake fasting, even if they tell themselves it's for their health. We feel clearer, lighter, "closer to the bone," after thinning ourselves out a bit (the meaning of the Aramaic word for fasting, *tsum*).

On another level, we may find we've painted ourselves into a proverbial corner due to the lies we've told ourselves, or the lies of others we agreed to accept, in order to live a comfortable, easy life. Yeshua could have stayed home in Galilee and lived in peace, all the while teaching people about *malkuta*, the "I Can" of vision-empowerment that is coming. From historical evidence, other "prophets" and "messiahs" were doing the same in his time. Yet to act upon *malkuta*, he needed to go to Jerusalem and disrupt things a bit.

Perhaps life is calling you now to face yourself clearly, to reevaluate what you tell yourself and what you agree to in life. What no longer rings true? What fills the heart with strength and purpose even if it brings some disruption? Has the gap between your heart's desire and your outer life become unmanageable? Are you longing for the balance of *khenuta*, which brings your inner world and outer world closer together? This can be an important turning point for you. Yeshua's life and teachings offer support for this pivot to a new life.

CONTEMPLATION

I breathe with the word "khe-noo-tah" resonating in and around my heart, adding a sense of need and urgency.

I feel my breath supported by that of Yeshua, who showed a way to fulfill one's purpose in life. I gaze through the eyes of the heart, breathing with as much love and thankfulness as I can feel for the way that my life has unfolded up to now. I know this is essential in order to move on. Only a heart that feels complete can see clearly (14).

If life is presenting me with a pressing need or with seemingly unreconcilable alternatives, I don't waste the opportunity. I allow the need to help open the window of my heart to see my self (naphsha) clearly, just as it is. At the same time, a new vision of outer reality is beginning to break through from my soul—the limitless possibility of Alaha.

CHAPTER THIRTEEN

Involuntary Love

Key Words: tubwayhun rahme

When you are drawn or guided to this day, allow a larger love to flow into and through you, a love not limited within the walls of your skin.

Could I volunteer to feel involuntary love? According to Yeshua, I can only choose to clear the way for such a love to "love through me." So how do I clear the way? In Matthew's Beatitudes Yeshua says that we can first find our real home in the breath (2). This leads to breathing with and feeling the emotional or mental sticky notes from the past that haunt me (21). My self then softens so that my soul can begin to save and heal me (23). Then I begin to really, truly, passionately want soul and self, *ruha* and *naphsha*, in balance in my heart—ripe, now (12). Step by step. Or all this can happen immediately, without steps. Birth happens, a miracle of life. Next in Matthew's Beatitudes, he says:

> *"In blissful happiness, at the right moment, are those through whom a flow of deep love streams; they are giving birth to new, never-before-seen life in themselves and others."**

---

* Matt. 5:7: "Blessed are the merciful: for they shall obtain mercy."

Roots and Branches

The words usually translated "merciful" and "mercy" here are *lamrahmane* and *rahme*, a love-word based on the ancient Semitic roots (RHM) used for the word "womb" (3). They show a streaming of light and heat (RA) from a deep place inside (HM). The HM root also tips us off that that Sacred Sense–Holy Wisdom *hakima* (H-KM-A) is here. This is no abstract idea of unconditional love, but one deeply felt, wordlessly, through all of our embodied senses.

Message for Today

Simple, right? Yes, so simple that there is nothing for us to do when such love appears except . . . let go. As I noted previously, however, getting there may lead us into many dark places within our personal self-*naphsha*. Yet deep within, our *naphsha* truly wants to release the ways it blocks the soul-*ruha's* flow. From these depths and darkness a flow of birth energy streams everything we could name as love, light, or life. In other words, everything we are looking for in the outer appearances of life, which only offer us temporary pleasure rather than a lasting touchstone of happiness.

One thing I have learned is that, having once felt this touchstone, even during bad days, I can feel thankfulness for the opportunity of life. The biggest pitfall may be feeling I need to hold onto any moment of happiness, thanks, or love, like Yeshua's students wanting to remain in the Mount of Transfiguration experience by building little huts to live there permanently. Surprise: the blissful vision of Yeshua and the prophets immediately disappeared. The flow of *rahme* comes with a new face every day.

Perhaps you and I are being called to give thanks before we receive, and most especially *as* we are receiving. We can give thanks not to our *naphsha*-self for creating a particularly wonderful relationship, experience, or accomplishment, but rather to the source of deep *rahme*, a love that rises from the depths underneath and within us.

CONTEMPLATION

Breathing "rah-hm-may" in the heart, I feel my breathing sinking lower, into the solar plexus, belly, root and through my hips, legs, and feet. Then even further into the center of the earth. There I can feel a deep *rahme*-birthing-love energy reflecting back up into me, embracing me with all the mother-love I could ever wish for.

As this breath from underneath again reaches my heart, I feel a small fire begin to grow there, burning up whatever memories of the past hold me captive. I place them all in this purifying fire. Then I throw in my own small sense of self, which rises from the ashes purified. Finally, I can begin to feel the possibility of real freedom.

I may return to this practice whenever I feel the need for it. Or I may also build up to it with the contemplations in the other Beatitude "steps" referenced earlier (see also appendix C.)

CHAPTER FOURTEEN

Seeing Life with a
Complete Heart

Key Words: dadkeyn blebhon, nehzun l'alaha

When you are guided or drawn to this day, feel your heart's deeply felt need to feel united and complete and to see your life clearly.

In the next Beatitude in Matthew, Yeshua offers the opportunity to feel completely *within heart*, seeing life lit up, outlined in light and clarity. This happens directly after we can feel our hearts overflow with love and thankfulness as part of the larger, birthing energy surrounding us in our *ruha*-soul's womb (13). Here we can connect heart, head, and all our senses to perceive the Larger Life everywhere:

*Full of joy, blissful in the now, are those who find themselves complete within their hearts; they shall be illuminated by signs of Reality wherever they look.**

Roots and Branches

The words usually translated "pure in heart" are *dadkeyn b'lebhon*, complete and full to overflowing *within* heart. Remember that ancient peoples felt that the heart in our flesh was an expression of an unseen reality of

---

* Matt. 5:8: "Blessed are the pure in heart: for they shall see God."

perception, thinking, feeling, loving, and willing. As noted earlier, there was no word for "mind" or "brain" in ancient Semitic languages. This explains Yeshua's saying usually translated, "out of the heart proceed unripe ('evil') thoughts" (Matt. 15:19). The words usually translated "see God" are the Aramaic *nehzun l'Alaha*: to have one's sight illuminated, as though in a lightning flash, by Reality itself.

Message for Today

The part of this saying about "seeing God" can remind us of the Holy One speaking to Moses in Exodus (33:20): "You cannot see my face, for no human being can see me and live." For the ancients, the "face" (*pana* in Hebrew) represented the essence of a person's expression in time and space. The Qur'an later speaks about *fana* (from the same Semitic roots), literally losing the outer face or appearance of something, with only the fullness of Reality's beauty and power remaining (55:26–27). When a little of that fullness pervades our hearts, then our small self, the *naphsha*, has little choice but to "pass away." In such moments, life passes before our eyes in clarity, as though in a flash of lightning, without any ability or need to impose our personal preferences on it.

Today, of course, the conventional view tells us that no one can really know the truth. Everything is relative points of view, nothing true or false. For Yeshua, when I view life from the flash of the heart's ray, what is actually happening before me becomes completely clear. Along with clear sight comes *malkuta*, the "I can" (10), revealing what is mine to do now.

Perhaps life is calling you to a pilgrimage on Yeshua's "Beatitude way": to first clear the heart of personal preferences, then allow it to fill up and overflow with thankfulness and love. Complete in heart we *can* see and think clearly. This is the proper use of the surface of the heart. Clearing our heart may happen in an instant, in a moment of deep need, or it may take several steps. However, neither can happen if we simply drift along, dozing or dosing our way through life because that's more comfortable than following the way Yeshua points out.

CONTEMPLATION

Returning to breathing within the heart, I again feel the movement of love and life downward from above my body all through it and then into the center of the earth. There I find another source of Big Love waiting to bounce back up through my lower body into the heart. I feel all the love and thankfulness I could ever have wished to receive from anyone. So from below and above, I am flooded with more than enough to feel complete.

Breathing in the phrase "dahd-kayn," complete, and out "b'leb-hon," within heart, the flow of life and love spreads from the heart around me.

Then breathing "neh-zoon 'l'alaha," I gaze through the heart at situations in my life now. The larger ray of love, which includes belly and heart together, can rise into the head so that my whole body becomes a heart. All my senses clear to show me the signs of what really is, as well as what is mine to do.

CHAPTER FIFTEEN

Gently Flows the Water of Peace

Key Words: abday, shlama, qara

*When you are drawn or guided to this day, take the opportunity
to feel yourself become a clear channel for love, light, and life,
which flows into your world, watering plants of universal peace.*

Planting is hard work, especially wherever digging is involved. But
there's also composting the soil: taking what we have not fully consumed
of life, letting it heat up, turning, adding more, turning again, keeping an
eye on it and the weather, then harvesting, and loading the heavy loam
into a bucket or barrow to grow more. We humans have been doing
something similar for ten thousand years or so. Then there is also the
"found agriculture" of those who preceded farmers, the hunter-gather-
ers, who also did deep work inwardly to intuit where to search as well
as undertake long journeys to find food. A few of us may have lived
in some sort of food paradise, but these paradises seem to have been
temporary and subject to "acts of god/dess," leading to briefer lifespans
than we experience today.

All this was known to Yeshua's listeners. So when he speaks of the project of planting universal peace in our lives, it also involves work, inner and
outer, as well as patience—the ability to make time (and impatience) stop.
By "universal peace," I mean the word Yeshua uses—*shlama*—the deep
peace that flows from Reality's spring through an open channel between

soul and self, *ruha* and *naphsha*. When this channel establishes itself on a regular basis, it grows the "peace that passes understanding" each season (Phil. 4:7). Again from Matthew's Beatitudes:

> "At the blessedly ripe moment is everyone who allows themselves to be living, perennial planters of peace, channels of Reality's creation moment. By hollowing themselves out (as the stalk of a plant allows nutrients to flow), they shall be engraved with the sign of Alaha, Reality itself."*

Roots and Branches

Besides *tubwayhun* (1), the key word here is *abday*, usually translated as the "makers" part of "peacemakers." Its roots show the seemingly paradoxical meanings of both bowing down and creating, of surrendering and consciously bringing forth the unseen. Planting brings all these into play. One bends over to plant, creating space inside oneself as one digs into the earth to allow growth to happen. The word translated "called" is a form of *qara*, which also reveals the image of engraving or hollowing out, creating a channel for the flow of light and radiance (QA+RA). We find a Hebrew form of the same word in Genesis 1 when the Holy One "calls," or engraves, creation into existence. "Children" is a form of *bna*, any birth, emanation, or new opening.

Message for Today

These are easy lessons to understand but difficult to enact, at least from my experience. There are times to work hard and other times to let nature take its course. Sometimes the hardest work is to simply hollow out the *naphsha*. Even though I am putting all of my personal energy into a project, I don't need to take it so personally. I can let go as I plant. Success or failure are defined by onlookers, who have their own ways of perceiving.

---

* Matt. 5:9: "Blessed are the peacemakers: for they shall be called the children of God."

Perhaps life is calling you to work harder, work more wisely, or stop outer work altogether for a while. Can you sense where the *ripeness* of your project (or your life) is at the moment? In which season it lives? Can you sense the ripeness of your own *naphsha* in this moment? This is the real plant that has its winters, summers, autumns, and springtimes. Can we keep our self's earth fertile by composting, heating, and transmuting past moments into present growth?

CONTEMPLATION

First I breathe in and around the heart with the words for planting peace—"ahb-dai shlah-mah." Can I surrender to the work necessary for keeping my heart open to the soul's inspiration and creative energy—including the inner work of letting go? This flow is the only plant that offers real peace and happiness as well as lets me be satisfied with whatever outcome happens.

Then letting go a bit more, I breathe in "d'al-la-ha" and out "net-qar-oon," feeling myself a channel for a larger Reality to flow through and then outward into my surroundings. The flow of *shlama* constantly changes and grows throughout my life. This is how I provide food for my *naphsha*, the bread of life it needs every season.

CHAPTER SIXTEEN

Begin Again in a Childlike Light

Key Words: shelu b'sheme

When you are guided to this day, take time to clear space within your heart. Then feel yourself instantly younger, bathed in a shower of unlimited light, love, and life.

Yeshua flips our usual script in so many ways. Usually we say we begin where we are, but he asks us to begin from a much larger, sensed experience of who we actually are: unlimited, connected light. With this type of beginning, we temporarily leave our usual, smaller sense of self (*naphsha*) behind. We reencounter it later, along with all of our life challenges, in a different way. When we have less of life's baggage to carry around, we feel instantly younger, more "spirited" (breathed). This is the simple key behind all of Yeshua's words about praying, healing, or asking for things "in his name." For instance:

> *"Whoever encounters and receives someone as a child, as though within my light and atmosphere, receives me at the same time."** *

---

* Matt. 18:5: "Whoso shall receive one such little child in my name receiveth me."

> *"If you open yourself to become a channel for my light and atmo-*
> *sphere, praying for something this way, it's as though I do it*
> *through you. So Abwun, the parent of the cosmos, sings a song*
> *through its child."*[†]

Roots and Branches

The phrase usually translated "in my name" is the Aramaic *b'sheme*. The first letter, *b*, can mean "with," "along with," "around," "in," or "within." So what is truly felt as though *within* is also felt around me—I find myself *within* a greater field of *shem*—light as vibration—a connected wave of inspiration, deep knowing, and wisdom. To "ask" or "pray" in Aramaic is a form of *shelu*, to open oneself and become empty, an instrument for a flow of this light-filled music. "Receive" is a form of *qabel*, to receive and perceive someone or something in time and space, material reality. "Glorify" is a form of *shebah*, a melody or song that returns to its source (24).

Message for Today

The real life is the connected life, says Yeshua. We are connected through light, vibration, and the music of life with the things and beings we perceive around us as well as with a much larger, unseen world. In both we can touch Yeshua's *shem*, his atmosphere. This atmosphere is not limited and does not limit anyone who touches it. On the contrary, it frees us to feel the same freedom and unlimited possibility that Yeshua himself felt, yet in our own way. We find the fulfillment of whatever we desire in this larger light-love-life field. We simply (simply!) need to burst the boundary of our small self-*naphsha*, our limited breath, and touch the soul-*ruha*, the Big Breath.

[†] John 14:13: "What ye shall ask in my name, I will do for you; that the Father may be glorified in his Son."

Perhaps now is the time for you to begin again, from a different center of seeing and doing. The larger music of life is really already present in *all* of our relationships—it's what we always yearn for—but we overlook that it's our soul, *ruha*, tapping us on the shoulder to remind us of this larger connection. Yeshua offers himself as one touchpoint, one place to connect *through*. He doesn't intend for us to stop with him but to go through him to the larger field of *shem*, which he called *shemaya*, a "heaven" that is simultaneously above, below, all around, and within us.

CONTEMPLATION

I feel my breathing rise and fall in a natural rhythm. Then I place one hand lightly over my chest, allowing my sense of body awareness or "center" to drop from my head and settle in and around my heart. At the same time, I feel my breathing become deeper and more relaxed.

Opening further, I use Yeshua's word "shel-oo," to become empty to receive. To help clear up the connection, I breathe "b-shem-ay" (within my *shem*), touching Yeshua's atmosphere. I avoid images, pictures, or thoughts about him, and keep breathing into a sensed, living connection, now, which is only freeing, not limiting.

Finally, breathing "shi-bah," I begin to feel my life simpler, younger, more harmonious—a song returning to its Source, *Abwun*.

CHAPTER SEVENTEEN

A Cloudy Eye

Key Words: ayna, heshukha, nuhra

When you are drawn or guided to this day, take the opportunity to clear persistent clouds from your inner vision so you can see what is really going on.

Images of ourselves or other people, memories, disappointed hopes—all these create impressions on the surface of our hearts. Some traditions counsel clearing this "mirror" constantly. Yeshua tells us that all these impressions appear simply as part of accepting the gift of being human. We can see them as an opportunity to practice letting go, in preparation for letting go of the stickiest image—that of having an individual self, a *naphsha*, which doesn't last more than the number of breaths we have in this body.

In one type of prayer-practice, we change our inner weather, dispersing each cloud on our heart, blowing it away. In another, we jump behind the clouds to realize that the sun is still shining: in other words, the sun of consciousness, our *ruha*-soul, which creates our small self, along with all its clouds. We human beings get what we—collectively and individually—perceive and then act upon. Yeshua uses both methods and expands a bit more on their nuances:

> *"Whenever the living spring of your heart's eye—inner and outer—gets clogged up, all of your senses become endarkened, clouded, obscured. The light that wants to come through from*

the soul's side is veiled, and inner light cannot touch outer light.
This is you reexperiencing the Great Darkness at the beginning
of the cosmos, before 'let there be light' became a reality. Before
consciousness—knowing and experiencing consciously—became
a possibility."*

Roots and Branches

The word translated "evil" is a form of *bisha*, unripeness—something not
at the right time and place, out of rhythm with the moment. "Darkness"
is *heshukha* (8), directly related to the Hebrew *hoshech*, which Genesis 1:2
uses to name the compacted, dense, unknowability of what was "before"
the beginning of the cosmos. "Light" is again a form of *nuhra*: inner and
outer light, knowing, wisdom, and the ability of the *naphsha*-self to experience itself. "Body" is really corpse, *pegra*. Aramaic does not have a
word for the form of a living "body," only its substance, the flesh (*besra'*).
Nothing is really living in us when the flow of *nuhra* from its source gets
stopped up.

Message for Today

We are infinite light seeking light, with our heart mediating a human
experience, one that offers a creative twist all our own to the years we
have in the flesh. Does this creativity equal true freedom? That is, can we
see, hear, and feel what has never existed before but is ripe for growing
what we are here to do now? That's our potential. Or have we become
so limited that we can't feel anything but our small self and its isolation
from everything and everyone around us? If so, "How great that darkness!" as Yeshua says, foreseeing how prevalent the feelings of alienation and despair would become in modern life.

Life is calling us to realize that we are all a bit "endarkened." And
equally that we can immediately clear the clouds. We have the full

---

* Matt. 6:23: "But if thine eye be evil, thy whole body shall be full of darkness.
If therefore the light that is in thee be darkness, how great is that darkness!"

support of the source of light and love that created our life. Each of us can actually change our own lives, and through this, the life of all other living beings with whom we are joined through our shared connection, *ruha d'qudsha*, Sacred Breath.

CONTEMPLATION

I begin by affirming that I don't need to follow the path that my family has determined, my memories have laid down, or the "weather" of my past predicts. I can change it. Then I breathe with a feeling of thankfulness in and around my heart: here I am, within the light of the soul supporting me.

Then I add the word "hesh-oo-kha," breathing with any unclarity I may feel. This could be something specific. Or I could take a moment to clear any impressions I am carrying from yesterday, or anytime in the past. There's space in breath and heart for them to arise now. To whatever arises, I add more and more light, "nooh-rah." Or I breathe out "hesh-oo-kha" and breathe in "nooh-rah," releasing any feeling of constriction from on or around my heart.

If something remains, I ask: What is this telling me? What amount of light, love, and thankfulness would transmute it entirely? Into the space of the question, I feel that amount of *nuhra* pouring in, and I accept the gift, as much as I need.

CHAPTER EIGHTEEN

Breathing Differently

Key Words: ruha d'qudsha, shubqana

When you are guided to this day, accept the opportunity to breathe differently: to feel your breathing like a sixth sense perceiving what your other five senses miss.

Sometimes we can have a feeling that someone behind us is looking at us. And they are. Or we wake up knowing that something particular will happen later in the day, even though it makes no logical sense. And it does. Or we have a feeling of communion with another person or an animal that cannot be explained. People have called this a "sixth sense" or by other names. According to Yeshua, what's important is that we don't deny the feeling of connectedness. It's real, and as near as our own breath. He says:

"By the earth on which I stand, I'm telling you the truth: all feelings of being cut off or tangled up can be released and untied, even lies and slander. But lying about, slandering, and denying—in words or actions—the existence of Sacred Breath: this cannot be untangled and returned to a healthy state while a person is living in their cut-off reality, acting as if only their small self exists."*

---

* Mark 3:28–29: "Verily I say unto you, all sins shall be forgiven unto the sons of men, and blasphemies wherewith soever they shall blaspheme. But he that shall blaspheme against the Holy Ghost hath never forgiveness but is in danger of eternal damnation."

Roots and Branches

"Holy Spirit" in Aramaic is *ruha d'qudsha*, more accurately "Sacred Breath." Even the equivalent phrase in the Greek version of this passage, *pneuma to hagion*, can be understood in the same way, as long as the Greek word *Theos* is understood in Yeshua's way: as Reality itself, rather than with the Platonic notion of a "God apart." The word translated "sins" is a form of the Aramaic *khatha*, a tangle or break in a connection (26). The word translated "blaspheme" is from the Aramaic *gudapha*, "to lie," "cause a break," or "slander." The words about forgiveness are forms of *shubqana*, to release or return something to its healthy, natural state (26).

Message for Today

Yeshua names an important understanding that is largely absent in Western culture today: there is one breath connecting the seen and unseen world. Today, humanity is just beginning to rediscover that we all breathe the same outer breath, from the same atmosphere, however polluted it may be around us. Yeshua counsels us to acclimate our *naphsha* to the healthy habit of breathing differently when we find ourselves feeling tangled up in a situation or cut off from our deeper inspiration. We can feel breathed by Reality rather than trapped within our skin. The individual self, the *naphsha*, is limited and contained within the *ruha*, a small "I" within the larger "I." This was better understood in Yeshua's time, especially by poor people who were often just "holding on" (9). Yet even in his time, the effects of wealth, privilege, and city culture had spread further through the region, and people were often forced to bow to these unhealthy, tangled influences wielded by political and religious officials.

Perhaps life is asking you to question your own sense of entitlement, of knowing more or better, or being more ethical than other people. These are the subtlest traps, which can lead to feeling trapped within our own small breath, quickly powerless, even when it would be ripe to speak out. Can we take the first step to question how comfortable we really feel ensconced in our own small sense of self, of breath? And then take the next step—to breathe differently?

CONTEMPLATION

I stop whatever I am doing for a few moments and breathe with the words "roo-hah d'qoodsha," in and out. Settling into my own natural breathing wave, I feel their open sounds settling and resonating in and around my heart.

Can I humble myself enough to ask for help to let go into this larger breath, one less confined by my own concerns, more open to a deeper sense of creativity, healing, and empowerment? Yeshua is always pointing me in this direction.

If some specific impression arises that constricts my breathing, I mix the sound of the word "shoob-qahn-ah" into it: releasing into healing emptiness. In the moment when emptiness and fullness, out-breath and in-breath merge, where all senses unite, *there—* Sacred Breath.

CHAPTER NINETEEN

New Wine in Old Wineskins

Key Words: hamra hadta

When you are drawn to this day, consider the opportunity to change your way of doing things to fit the new, passionate realization that is warming and fermenting within you.

Sometimes life presents us with a surprise—an illness, the breakup of a relationship, a dramatic escape from danger, a seemingly miraculous healing, an unexpected gift, or an inner awakening, just to name a few. When Yeshua would heal someone, he would often tell them to "go home another way." Why? Because the people who know us best (as the "sick one," the "needy one," etc.) can often unconsciously hold onto this image while we are changing or may have already changed. He puts it another way in the famous saying about putting new wine in old wineskins:

> *"No one places fresh, fermenting wine, still on the way to giving happiness, into skins that are on their way to disintegration. The fermenting wine will burst the old sack because it no longer has flexibility, and the wine runs out. So people put new wine into new wine skins, and the one guards the other."**

---

* Matt. 9:17: "Neither do men put new wine into old bottles: else the bottles break, and the wine runneth out, and the bottles perish: but they put new wine into new bottles, and both are preserved." Also Mark 2:22, Luke 5:37.

Roots and Branches

Aramaic has two words for "wine"; the one here is *hamra*, pointing from its roots to something that warms, envelops, generates passion. The word for "new" is a form of *hadta*, based on the root HD, for something that is lively, at its beginning stage, giving happiness or unfolding in specific, guided way (32). Related to this word, one of the "beautiful names of Allah" in the Qur'an becomes *Al Hadi*. Today wine is aged in bottles or barrels, but then sacks made of skin were used, and if they were too old, the fermenting wine would split them and both wine and skin would be lost.

Message for Today

Yeshua recognized that, when something is fermenting in us—a new wine, a new realization of life—our outer life needs to change. The Jerusalem Temple rituals of his time had for generations been co-opted by whichever political regime held power. Their inner ability to reunite a person's soul with their self, *ruha* with *naphsha*, their power to warm a person's heart and revive their passion, had withered. He brought something new: the realization that *every* person's "I" could reunite directly with the ultimate source of its renewal. The individual, personal "I" could ferment into a new, transformed "I" by connecting to its origin: I to I, one to One. The Gospel of John quotes Yeshua using the formula "I-I" (*ina ina*) numerous times in various sayings mistranslated, for instance, as "I am the way, the truth and the life."[†] This fermentation required new containers. So Yeshua acted as a spiritual disrupter rather than a person attempting to reform ways that had succumbed to (in today's terms) "spiritual materialism."

Nearly fifty years ago, when I was an investigative reporter, I was pursuing a story that took me from Colorado to the West Coast. On a ride share (I was young!), the car flipped over in the middle of the Great

---

† See the second half of RAJ for these translations.

Salt Lake Desert in Utah. Somehow, we all were unharmed, flipped the car back over, taped the windshield on, and continued on our way. I was deeply shaken, inside and out. The next week I met my spiritual guide for the first time in California, and I was open enough to experience a bit of the transmission of light that he offered through his eyes. It was a breakdown followed by a breakthrough, and it changed my life.

Perhaps life is calling you now to pivot to a new way of living, one more suited to the breakthrough or breakout you have recently experienced. Guided by grace, these opportunities offer us a way to drink the wine of being more fully human, embodying life with an increase of satisfaction, passion, and happiness. Consider the gift, and if you hear this call, accept it.

CONTEMPLATION

Breathing in "ham-rah," passionate warmth, and breathing out "had-ta," joyful guidance, I feel my heart open to unexpected possibilities around me.

At the same time, I experience a new, inner opening as my heart connects my small self "I" with the source of love, healing, life, grace, light—the only "I," which welcomes me into my *soul's* embrace.

Grace has brought me to this peak moment and warmed my heart. It promises to ferment my enfleshed life so that it can become intoxicatingly happy.

CHAPTER TWENTY

A Rest Stop Between Here and There

Key Words: alaha, nyach

When you are drawn or guided to this day, accept the gift of taking a pause from your daily activities to rest in an easy, natural breath felt in and around your heart.

"Taking time out" has become a phrase that everyone now understands, from children to adults. But from *what* are we taking time and where is the "out"? Modern life seems to be an endless series of things to do, of doings. We seem to have no control over our sense of time when we only experience one thing after another. Taking time for oneself again begs the question, which self? Does it simply mean letting my thoughts, worries, and anticipatory fears about the future run wild? Probably this, more than anything, is what keeps us all busy, rushing from one thing to another, even on a holiday.

Yeshua proposes that we stop time itself by first taking regular moments to rest the small self, the *naphsha,* and second to discover a deeper resting-place in the middle of the wave of our breathing, between the in-breath and the out-breath. This is not unique to his teaching and is found in many ancient spiritual traditions worldwide. Yet he has a simple, beautiful way of expressing it:

"Come toward my way, everyone who is weary from carrying burdens that either weigh you down or prevent you from moving

*onward in your life. I offer you a way to lay them all down, to
pause in the middle of up and down, back and forth. . . . My
work is: planting the light in your self. A very small burden,
aromatic, delightful to all your senses."**

Roots and Branches

Whenever Jesus talks about "coming to me," he means coming to his
way of living and experiencing reality. Here this phrase is the Aramaic
taw lawoty. The key word in this saying, translated "rest," is a form of
nyach, from the old Semitic roots NCh or NH. These roots also com-
pose the name of the biblical prophet Noah (*Nu(c)h* in Aramaic). The
rest we are supposed to find is like the ark in which Noah rides out the
world-destroying flood. What threatens to flood us are our burdens,
a form of *mawbala* (the KJV renders this "heavy laden"), which weigh
our small self down, preventing us from moving. The word translated
"yoke" (*nira*) relates to both planting as well as embodying the light as
a lamp. The word translated "easy" (a form of *basiym*) can also mean
"spicy," "delightful," and "aromatic," all words relating to both planting
and what pleases our senses.

Message for Today

Our real lifework is receiving the light of our soul (*ruha*) through our
heart, then planting it in our self (*naphsha*) and embodying it. Again,
some digging is often required (15). Some of this goes on in our sleep
and dreams, where healing and inspiration can arrive, then become
embodied the next morning. Ancient peoples saw seeds as living beings
waiting to receive their proper place for "rest"; then with ripe timing and
nurturing, they reveal a freshly embodied form of light, some of which
we humans can receive as food.

---

* Matt. 11:28, 30: "Come unto me all ye that labour and are heavy laden, and I
will give you rest. . . . For my yoke is easy and my burden is light."

Perhaps life is calling you to enter this deep place of rest, plant a seed received in your heart, and grow a new life filled with more love than before. This resting place may be as near as your own breath.

CONTEMPLATION

Closing my eyes, I rest for a moment, feeling a natural, easy breath centered in and around my heart. I begin to breathe in hearing "Ala-ha," Reality, and out "nee-yach." Reality is resting and renewing through me.

I begin to notice the brief pauses that occur naturally when my breath is all in or all out. Can I feel rest and renewal in these pauses? They are like the pause that nature goes through during winter, preparing for the spring. My breath and life are part of the same natural cycles.

I can also do this simple breathing attunement before going to sleep at night. Entering another, unseen reality, I feel supported by breathing, heartbeat, and a connection to *Alaha*. Nothing else is needed.

CHAPTER TWENTY-ONE

Rising Out of the Bottomless Pit

Key Words: tubwayhun, abiyla, biya

When you are guided here, take the opportunity to feel your soul healing whatever confusion and grief the surface of your heart is holding. Falling, you are lifted up again.

When the props with which we maintain our small self disappear—our identities, concepts, self-images, and accomplishments—we can feel as though we're falling into a bottomless pit. This is why so many people don't stop to breathe more deeply: they might begin to feel this sensation. The small self is ultimately temporary, which also is why confronting death, either that of a close one, or the remembrance of our own, can trigger a crisis.

Yeshua knew this very well, had experienced it himself, and made it part of his Beatitude way as reported in Matthew. After finding our home in the breath, really our *only* home (2), we may find our other temporary houses crumbling. He says:

> *"Blessedly ripe are those who feel themselves falling into a bottomless pit of confusion and grief. By allowing their soul to catch them, they will find a new home that comforts and lifts them, satisfying all desires."**

---

* Matt. 5:4: "Blessed are they that mourn: for they shall be comforted."

Roots and Branches

As we have seen, the word for "blessed are those" is *tubwayhun*, a form of *taba*, ripeness, being in tune with the heartbeat of our soul, and so Reality itself (2). At such moments we feel we are fulfilling our human purpose. This blessed ripeness often begins by shedding everything except the connection between our small breath with the Big Breath. "Mourn" is a form of *abiyla*, the roots of which (AB+LA) show an opening into a bottomless pit, which includes neglect, weakness, want, mourning, and nothingness—the feeling that nothing matters, and everything is an illusion. Of course, our small self-*naphsha* can feel this, since without feeling a connection to the *ruha*-soul, nothing else is left. To reconnect with it is *biya*, the root of the word translated as "comforted." It's all about moving beyond a sense of isolation, relocating from a "no" (LA) about life into a new home that has windows opening into the soul and Reality itself (B+YA).

Message for Today

In Yeshua's view, even difficult, bleak feelings point the way toward wholeness. Falling into a pit can result in being caught by the healing arms of the soul and being lifted up again. We can find that going down can lead to going up, since on the way we let go of the weight of the baggage pulling us down.

Perhaps life is calling you to stop for a moment and, breathing in the heart, feel what you have been neglecting. Even if it's only a "thought experiment," or really a "feeling experiment," imagine yourself shedding the identifications that are causing you confusion and grief, including the feeling that "nothing matters." If nothing mattered, you would not be here, now. But your *ruha*-soul brought you here for a purpose. If you can trust this, then what your heart perceives, imagines, and does matters to every heart and soul.

CONTEMPLATION

I begin by returning to breathing "too-bway-hoon," sensing only heartbeat and breathing in and around my heart.

Then I again feel my heart as a mirror and notice what appears in it that I have been overlooking or not feeling. I help this process along by breathing the sound "ah-bee-lah," confusion, grief, bottomlessness. After a few breaths, I begin to bring in the sound and feeling "bee-yah," comfort, feeling myself rising up. I have released the sound "la," which means "no," and what's left is not only a "yes," but the Big Yes!—a form of the "unnamable name" in the tradition, *Yah*. Really, it's the sound of my own breath that I experience as part of Holy Breath, sacred spirit.

CHAPTER TWENTY-TWO

Tied Up, Released

Key Words: asiyr, shra

When you are drawn or guided to this day, take the opportunity to feel the inner "muscles" of your heart able to both hold and release, to gather and scatter, to feel a circle closing as well as opening: heart flexibility.

Thomas Jefferson once said, "The government you elect is the government you deserve." A native Middle Eastern mystic like Yeshua would say, "We get the world we perceive, then handle and act upon according to the way it appears to us." If our *ruha*-soul is the ultimate viewer, seeing through the eyes of our heart, then the extra spin or coloring we add is our own *naphsha* drawing together or releasing, gathering or scattering the bits we call thoughts interweaving with the way material reality appears.

Because our soul is very cooperative, it gives us what the heart chooses, even or especially if we're not aware of choosing. This goes for our collective human *naphsha* as well. The only way to change this is to go into the realm of *ruha*, which is that of connected light, love, and life energy—"heaven." Go higher and deeper to the Source, *Alaha*. Yeshua comments:

"If your heart chooses to enclose a part of itself in a circle of material stuff, then that part is closed off to your soul, the world of light and connectedness, shemaya.

> *If your heart chooses to release that circle and untie part of its occupation with material stuff, that same heart-portion will open to and make its home in shemaya."**

Roots and Branches

The words translated "bind" and "loose" are complementary in Aramaic: one means a circle closing, *asiyr*; the other a circle opening, or a straight line being freed from being enclosed, *shra*, also related to *shrara* (8). "Earth" is a form of *ar`ah*, any form of individual, particle-reality, material existence, including nature. "Heaven" is *shemaya* (5), the connected wave and sound reality of existence.

Message for Today

There is nothing negative about either binding or loosing in Yeshua's saying. They are both forms of light, *nuhra*—one enfleshed, the other not. He's simply reminding us of the way our consciousness works. If we don't like what we're tangled up in, we can change it. We only need to go higher and deeper, to the source of light, the always-on, 24/7 awareness of the soul-*ruha*. This is what all healthy meditation, prayer, and ritual are about. We will feel more free when we discover we can connect this way; a portion of our heart-mind awareness will be living in *shemaya* all the time. No one needs to give us permission or any special status to do it. The connection between self and soul through the heart is always there, part of our human heritage. We only need to clear enough heart space to let the light from the Beginning radiate through. We can then take up the "binding" part again, acting in embodied life in a new, hopefully more ripe way.

Perhaps life is calling you to take a moment to release and at the same time—instantly—feel free and connected with the inspiration

---

* Matt. 18:18: "Whatsoever ye shall bind on earth shall be bound in heaven: and whatsoever ye shall loose on earth shall be loosed in heaven."

needed to go forward in life. To clear your heart's surface as well as let healing and love break through. Take a moment to do so.

CONTEMPLATION

Breathing an easy, natural breath in and around the heart, I again relax into this feeling as my real home. I notice any restrictions, obsessions, or painful feelings that arise, and at the same time I release them in all times—past, present, and future.

I help the process by breathing in "as-eer"—binding—and breathing out "shrah"—releasing. I add more light and love. I feel my heart now more able to both hold and release, to tie and untie, to feel entangled and free. In this life, the one cannot exist without the other. I open space for whatever quality of light and love I need now to free myself from unhelpful habits or painful memories of the past. I don't need to focus on or even remember them.

My "heart-muscle" may need some extra massage oil, so I add thankfulness. Thankful that I am here, able to do just what I am doing—breaking out of jail to my new home in the cosmos.

CHAPTER TWENTY-THREE

What Could Be Softer?

Key Words: makikhe, nertun ar`ah

When you are guided to this day, accept the opportunity to feel any place in your body that may be too tense or rigid to receive your natural inheritance, the gifts of nature: well-being and health.

"Life is hard. Be tough. Be resilient. Prepare for the worst." No doubt there are many reasons to be pessimistic if one only receives the so-called news that is broadcast over television or the internet. But what about the real news—in the form of our *ruha*-soul's simulcast that is streaming to us health, life, healing, strength, and every other quality that we tend to look for only in what we perceive around us?

In his Beatitude way in Matthew, Yeshua recommends following our experience of confusion, lack of direction, and hopelessness (21) with a deeper breath, one connected with nature, which frees us from the rigidity armoring us against our natural happiness:

"Tuned to the Source and happy in ripeness are those who consciously soften what is too rigid within them. They are receiving their natural inheritance of strength and healing from the gift of being part of nature's world, of being enfleshed in time and space."*

---

* Matt. 5:5: "Blessed are the meek: for they shall inherit the earth."

Roots and Branches

After *tubwyahun*, blessed ripeness (2), the key word *makikhe*, usually translated "meek," means to soften what is too rigid in our flesh, heart, or *naphsha*-self. Only then are we ripe for receiving our natural inheritance (*nertun*)—not a piece of material property, but strength and vitality, the meanings of the roots of *nertun* (N, AR, T). The word usually translated "earth," *ar`ah*, does not mean the world or even only the planet Earth. It points to all of nature and our own heritage as beings in the natural world, inheritors of the gifts from mineral, plant, and animal—the beings created before us.

Message for Today

Yes, there are times to be tough and resilient, to allow things to bounce off us. But is that time now for you? Is there a way that you often find yourself wallowing in self-pity rather than really softening what is preventing you from receiving help from another self or nature, the unseen world (which some call angelic healing), or the Source of healing itself? All are absolutely real. Reality is constantly knocking on our door, gently tapping us on the shoulder, asking "What could be softer?"

Every step of the Beatitude way in Matthew is a moment we experience in time and space, a doorway to something both within and beyond them. Perhaps now is your time to feel Yeshua's step three: softening to receive strength. Or you might feel drawn to read or revisit the first two steps (2, 21) and then return to this one. As Yeshua emphasizes throughout his teaching and actions, less *naphsha* allows more *ruha* to come through—more of the soul's illuminating, inspiring activity. This can refresh all dimensions of your life.

CONTEMPLATION

Breathing first the word "mah-kee-kay," softening, I turn within and feel places that could be softer. Where do I feel them in my body? What emotions are connected with them, and what was the earliest I felt them in life? Are they ready to be softened and released, in all times?

If I encounter many past impressions that need to be released, I open further, wider, and deeper from the heart, to receive strength from all around me. I lean into Yeshua's words on my in-breath "ner-toon" and breathe out "ar`ah." I sigh into the end of the word "ar`ah," a real "ahh!"

I am not better—or worse—than any other human being. I am connected with every other human being. And I am also a living, natural being, temporarily here as part of the natural world. As Genesis 1:26–27 says, I am destined to manage my individuality along with and within all the natural beings created before me.[†] This is my simple, human job description: the divine "image" embedded in me from the beginning.

---

† A phrase perversely mistranslated from the Hebrew as "be fruitful, multiply, dominate and subdue the earth and rule over [the beings created before us]." For more on this, see DW.

CHAPTER TWENTY-FOUR

Offer It All Up

Key Words: malkuta, hayye, shebah

*When you are drawn here, take the opportunity to dedicate
and fully release everything you do today toward the Source of
your life, Alaha—the larger vision, energy, and glorious song.*

When the fruit is ready, it falls from the tree. Sometimes it's eaten by a
human or other being. Other times it's absorbed by the earth, where its
outer flesh feeds the soil and all its micro-organisms, and its seed may
grow a new tree. In either case, the tree lets go so that another cycle of
life can continue. This is why Yeshua talks about a "ripe tree" bearing
ripe fruit as the way we are meant to live (Matt. 7:17, see HG). Unfortu-
nately, this passage is usually mistranslated with words like "good tree"
and "evil tree." Since we're human beings now and not trees, it's difficult
for us to let go of the fruit we have produced (even or especially if that
fruit is not very sweet). Yet imagine a tree that never let go. The wavelet
of life that produced it wouldn't last beyond its first form.

Yeshua finishes the simple prayer he offers to his students in Matthew with these words:

*"In You, from You, lives all of the original vision and power, the
life energy now, plus the melody of everything, a song returning
to the heart of the cosmos, age to age, world to world, time to
time. May I trust this ground of truth and live from here."**

---

* Matt. 6:13: "For thine is the kingdom, and the power, and the glory, for ever.
Amen."

Roots and Branches

"For thine" is *metol* (because) *dilakhe*, to you belongs or of you is existing. We have seen "kingdom" (*malkuta*) before—the vision and empowerment that allow us to say "I can" to anything (1). "Power" here is *hayla*, a form of *hayye*, life energy (8). "Glory" is a form of *sheba*, also a "song," (16) a word related to the one Genesis 1 uses to describe Elohim "returning" to itself (often translated "rested") during the seventh day (*sheboth*, later "Sabbath") of creation. The ancients viewed their individual lives as an ongoing melody, which flowed through the instrument of "I" for a period of time, continuing from a pre-birth past and then returning after physical death to a cosmic music, and further on. "For ever" is the Aramaic *l'ahlam almin*, literally from one level, time, gathering, or world to another. Other worlds, other lives, all inclusive. "Amen" is *ameyn*, its roots pointing to trust and faith, literally standing on and for something, as firmly as I believe I stand on the earth.

Message for Today

Yeshua continually challenges us to let go, particularly of things, projects, and processes that are weighing us down and have become rotten on the vine. "Ripeness is all," as Edgar says in Shakespeare's play. If we let go at the right time, then we either trust that a hand will be there to receive what we've offered, or what we have completed will fertilize growth in the future. We don't always need to learn a lesson consciously from every experience. We can trust that what happened is accepted by our soul-*ruha*. It is our soul that allows us to hear the ongoing melody and to feel that we are part of a bigger music, beyond words or concepts.

Perhaps now is the time to take a sabbath and return, turn within, whirl around a bit, and let go of whatever wants to be released. Trust that your soul will be there to catch you and provide the vision, life energy, and song to carry you further.

CONTEMPLATION

I again breathe naturally with an easy feeling in and around my heart. First, I bring in the feeling of releasing together with dedicating whatever has happened or been accomplished. This is the most important part. Aiding this, I breathe with these sounds: "mi-tol" (because) on the in-breath, and on the out-breath, "di-lakh-hey" (belongs). Why offer it all up? Because it's all existing in and belongs to the greater Reality anyway. We're just letting our *naphsha* acknowledge it.

Then I expand to include my whole life to this moment. Breathing "mal-koo-tah" in and out, I open to the vision and empowerment that brought me here, through various life experiences.

Then "hay-lah," feeling the life energy I need all around me. Finally "shi-bah," the song. Can I feel my own breathing and heartbeat as the melody and rhythm of my life? Can I open to the one sound within all the sounds I can take in right now? I bathe in that one sound and breath as my heart turns and returns to the home of its soul.

CHAPTER TWENTY-FIVE

Knocking on the Door of the Heart

Key Words: qush, eth-phetah

When you are drawn or guided to this day, take the opportunity to feel your heart resonant, responsive, and spacious—like a drum on which you can play a rhythm you've never heard before.

"My life is very full." I often hear this statement and want to ask, "Is that a good thing for you?" Is there no room for the unexpected, the unimagined, the previously self-defined "impossible"?

The point of knocking on a door is to be heard. The more hollow the door, the louder and more resonant is the sound of the knock. Think concrete instead of wood—nothing would be heard inside. Jesus compares this to the process of desiring what we don't have: we first need to hollow ourselves out, to prepare space for the "knock," and just as importantly, to envision the door opening. He expands on this by saying:

"Open yourself like a channel for the water of your desire; you will see love's fruit.

"Allow your inner gnawing emptiness to really empty you, making space for the fire of fulfillment.

"Knock and hollow your self, release hopes and fears. After contraction comes expansion, after closing comes opening."

Roots and Branches

All of the meanings of "ask," "seek," and "knock" in Aramaic (*shelu, be'uh, qush*) center around clearing our heart or hollowing out our self. All of the words for "given," "find," and "opened" in Aramaic (forms of *yahb, shkach, phetah*) relate to transforming this emptiness, lack of expectation, and hollow resonance into love's fruit, fire, and music (for more on this saying, see DW.)

Message for Today

The concept is easy to grasp in the abstract, but enacting it requires some digging in our hearts, some weeding and clearing space (15). Or we may need to release our full to overflowing hands so they can receive something new (20). Or soften the rigidity in our hearts that keeps us from resonating with any of life's unexpected music (23). Yeshua offers us many different images throughout his teaching. They spiral around the cultivation of the heart as living earth in which the self is planted. If it receives the proper weather and nutrients, from below and above, the seen and unseen worlds, then it bears fruit, flowers, and more life.

Perhaps life is calling you to create inner space for unexpected, seemingly impossible, heart visions to fulfill themselves. This requires a consistent willingness to ignore the unhelpful messages of our *naphsha's* voice, which often reminds us of what happened in the past, particularly what went wrong.

---

* Matt. 7:7: "Ask, and it shall be given you; seek and ye shall find; knock, and it shall be opened unto you."

CONTEMPLATION

I settle again and breathe with a sense of love and thankfulness in and around my heart. I am here, present. The face of my soul, the heart's real beloved, is always ready to meet me. Then I add the word "qoosh" (knock, hollow) on my inhalation and "eth-phetah" (be opened) on my exhalation. I slow down my breathing until this becomes easy. I notice which word feels lighter or easier to breathe: knocking or opening? Then I return to breathing only with that one for a while.

Sometimes I find myself happy to keep asking, but I find I don't really want to receive. Or vice versa. So I begin to breathe with the feeling of both knocking on the door and the door opening. I find this can reveal much about the way I am living my life at the moment. Being hollowed as I knock, I expect an opening. "If you don't shut down these natural movements by holding onto the past or anticipating the future," my soul tells me, "this is the way embodied life works. When you knock on the door of your heart, it opens easily, and you can meet the face of satisfied desire."

CHAPTER TWENTY-SIX

Untangling

Key Words: shbuqlan khtahayn

> *When you are drawn to this day, take the opportunity to*
> *unwind yourself from past events, situations, and relationships*
> *that prevent you from feeling your heart's joy. At the same time,*
> *untie others who are overly dependent on you, whether in the*
> *attitude of praise or blame.*

Debt, repayment, and forgiveness of debt have become major issues in the economies of the Western world. Who really owes what to whom for a past promise or the breaking of one? Some negative effects (like colonialism or pollution) have impoverished whole cultures for centuries. A great deal of messy untangling is necessary. Forgiving debt was also a huge issue in Yeshua's time. Virtually all of his listeners were considered debtors by the very small wealthy class that, in collusion with the Roman Empire, dominated the area. Ancient nomads, on the other hand, practiced the periodic forgiving of all debt for the maintenance of a healthy community. We see this in the celebration of the "jubilee year" mentioned in the Torah.

We can see the same process reflected on a personal level. We hold onto emotional capital or debt based on our past relationships with certain people or from past events. Starting where I am, which is the only sphere in which I have any real choice, can I release some of these threads, knots, and tangles, which restrict the freedom of my heart to connect to my soul? In Luke's version of Yeshua's prayer we find:

"Untangle the knots that compress my heart, making it rigid,
unable to return to its original flowing state. As I release my
end of a cord, the other end releases too."*

Roots and Branches

"Forgive" here is *shbuqlan* a form of *shubqana* (18), to release or return to
its original state (the root ShB) something that has become fixed, rigid,
or held in an unnatural way (-UQ). "Sins," a form of *khtahayn*, is based
on a root that points to the process of sewing, weaving, and mending—
meaning here the tangled threads in a relationship. Matthew's version
of the prayer uses a different word, one that points to trespassing or
stealing. Both versions use the Aramaic word *aykana* (usually translated
as "for" or "just as") meaning that, for our soul, releasing and being
released happen at the same time, rather than as a condition. So as I
release, I am released, and vice versa.

Message for Today

Both untangling and being untangled may happen simultaneously, but
the results don't always appear in the same moment as we measure time
and space—in days, hours, or seconds. Ancient peoples knew this. So
nomadic life was a continual process of clearing relationships and discovering what promises (a form of debt) could and should be released
for a heart to return to its healthy state.

Noticing the releasing can happen over time, or it can happen all
at once. If we first connect to our soul-*ruha*, we can download all the
love, life, and light that are already ours, this moment, if we make space
for them. This fire of love consumes all unhealthy cords and knots,
now. How much *do* we want this? Some threads cause people to be
dependent on us, but in an unhealthy way. Do we want or need this

---

* Luke 11:4: "And forgive us our sins; for we also forgive every one that is
indebted to us."

dependency to shore up our diminished sense of personal self, that is, our *naphsha*? Can we find self-acknowledgment in a more ripe way, as our soul opens to new vistas of what life can be for us without these ties?

Perhaps it's time to do some inner housekeeping. Has life become so cluttered with past emotional promises, debts, credits, and balance sheets that the accounting is eating up all the time you have to live joyfully, really free, in tune with the heart? If so, then spend some time with the following contemplation.

CONTEMPLATION

I breathe again with a feeling of ease in and around my heart, opening to my birthright of love and joy. Then I bring the word "shbuq-lahn" (release) into my in-breath and "kha-ta-heyn" (tangles) into my out-breath.

If any feeling of restriction arises in my heart, I release this first by opening to more love—above, around, and underneath me. I sit in the middle of a fire of love and feel all of the shackles of the past burn away. All the cords tying up my heart are releasing, now.

CHAPTER TWENTY-SEVEN

Checked Out? Recheck In!

Key Words: nesyuna, dakhra

*When you are guided here, accept the opportunity to be more
mindful of what your heart wants any time you have a choice
or decision to make today.*

Both *mindfulness* and *heartfulness* are words that have usefully entered
our vocabulary. One could say charitably that these have arisen because
the last few generations of so-called modern people are mostly checked
out—at the minimum checked out of their emotions, and at the maximum checked out of why they are actually doing anything. Even when
we feel we have no choice, we still have a choice to keep our heart open
to our soul and download the light and life that would clarify how to
either persevere or change course. In Yeshua's prayer, one of the most
misunderstood lines is:

"And don't let us enter forgetfulness, but free us from unripeness."*

Roots and Branches

As I have written about for more than forty years, the Aramaic words
la tahlan mean "don't let us enter" rather than "lead us not." Even the
Greek version, *mē eisenegkēs*, can mean "don't allow us to fall or enter."
"Temptation" is *nesyuna*, meaning literally forgetfulness. The opposite, to

---

* Matt. 6:13: "And lead us not into temptation, but deliver us from evil."

remember, is *dakhra*. These words point to a forgetfulness and remembrance of the limited time we have in the flesh, as well as of our origin before birth and our destination after physical death. "Deliver us" is *patsan*, based on a verb meaning "to free, release, or break a restriction." We saw the Aramaic for "evil," *bisha*, meaning unripeness, on several previous days (17).

Message for Today

Being forgetful of the gift of a limited lifespan and not being in the moment, in tune with our soul's timing and guidance, are two of the mental-emotional viruses of our time. Yeshua foresaw this human trend, so these lines of his prayer, rather than being an artifact of antiquated theology, actually point to the greatest challenge facing humanity now. Can we remember and act ripely, for the benefit of the greater human community as well as the community of nature upon which our bodies are intimately dependent?

Change begins not in large social movements, but with our own life and willingness to check in rather than be checked out so often. At the same time, we have to ward against merely accepting the abstract idea of Yeshua's saying without actually putting it into practice and acknowledging that forgetfulness also comes with the human job description. If we did not have the soul's freedom to forget, we would not be able to *choose* to remember on the level that Yeshua is talking about. Outer material life is very cooperative. It will provide us with the love, joy, and happiness that our *ruha*-soul feels, or with the opposite, which our all-too-forgetful *naphsha* expects.

Perhaps it's time to check back in, to expect a different outcome. This begins, as does most of Yeshua's way, with opening our hearts to our soul's unlimited source of love, which frees us to make choices not based on past regrets or future fears, not on what is most *bisha* in our personal or cultural life. Yes, *bisha* will still be around, so judging others by our own fixed standards can be just another path to forgetfulness.

CONTEMPLATION

I begin by focusing on the first two key words in Yeshua's saying. Feeling my heart, I breathe in and out the Aramaic "nes-yoo-nah," forgetfulness, distraction. I open my heart further to accept that this, as well as my personal self, is part of the human condition.

Then after a short time, I change the word on my out-breath to "da-khra," remember. I allow my heart to feel first one then the other. Gradually I feel my heart bringing both into balance and stillness. At this point of balance, I consciously choose the "remember" side, only breathing "da-khra." More fresh air pours through the window of my heart from the source of life and breath, *ruha*.

The words gradually dissolve, and I begin to feel my own breath as the prayer, the practice, the affirmation. I can make a deal with my *naphsha* that when I need to check in again, having momentarily checked out, the words will come into my heart to bring me back to balance in an instant.

CHAPTER TWENTY-EIGHT

Losing and Finding
Your Self

Key Words: shkach, abad

When you land on this day, take the opportunity to temporarily unwind some of your commitments to outer things and projects in order to find deeper repose within your soul's presence.

Our *naphsha*-self can feel very enmeshed with life's many engaging things. This is as it should be. We human beings would not have an individual self unless its purpose were to follow our heart's freedom—to choose love and life instead of the opposite. Yet sometimes, looking only outwardly, we can lose the plot of why we are doing what we're doing. This outwardness can include not only things, projects, and relationships, but also abstract ideas, philosophies of life, and spiritual searching. Are we searching just to search? If so, then all we will find is the face of our personal self reflected back to us. Yeshua puts it this way:

> *"Whoever envelops themselves fully in the small self-naphsha will find only restriction and shrouds covering their ruha-soul. Yet whoever feels the small self as a part of the whole, as a particle in Reality's wave of love, will find the deeper repose they are looking for. This is how to follow my way."**

---

* Matt. 10:39: "He that findeth his life shall lose it: and he that loseth his life for my sake shall find it."

Roots and Branches

Expanding the key Aramaic words used here: "Find" is a form of *shkach*, to envelop, shroud, surround, restrict, or find repose (25). "Lose" is a form of *abad*: a progression (shown in the Semitic root A) from feeling oneself particular, only a particle, an individual (BD), which ultimately leads to a sense of isolation. "Self" is *naphsha*, the individual breath and self we have seen many times. "For my sake," *metol* here means for following my way or example.

Message for Today

The question comes down to this: What are we really looking for in life? If it is only confirmation that our own small self is worth something, then the best way to follow that goal is to "find" our self as part of a larger whole, says Yeshua. This larger whole is the always-on, open 24/7, soul-breath, *ruha*. It allows me to find happiness, love, joy, and everything else I'm looking for, whether inside or out. This doesn't mean that I ignore daily life or consider it worthless. It means that I pursue what I do with a whole heart, one that is open to "both sides now"—*naphsha* and *ruha*. In the Gospel of Thomas, Yeshua offers a parallel commentary on the preceding, saying:

> "Whoever has come to really know the outer world, composed
> only of levels of time and space, has fallen over a corpse. And
> whoever has tripped over this corpse does not find such a world
> worth their while." (Thom. 56:1–2)

We do not want to go through life tripping over our own past memories, self-images, outdated promises, or habits that no longer serve us. We then become so enveloped and enervated that life no longer seems fresh and worth living. Find the presence and repose of the self in your deepest heart, the connection with the soul, says Yeshua. Practice it regularly. Then no matter what you do in life, that indwelling "found" presence (later called *Shekhina* in the Kabbalistic tradition) will be yours.

Perhaps life is calling you to thoroughly reevaluate everything you're caught up in right now. How much of it really speaks to your heart and soul? How much is just you going through the motions because you became accustomed to do so and are afraid of disappointing other people? Best lose some (or all) of that in order to find the joy of what's real now.

CONTEMPLATION

I begin again by breathing an easy, natural breath in and around the heart. I connect first with my source of love, life, and light, *ruha*. It's above, below, and all around me. I trust that it is there. Then I notice anything weighing on or enshrouding my heart, preventing more love and life from entering.

I ask that my soul help me release anything unnecessary into the light, without judgment. Breathing out "ab-ahd," I lose whatever I don't need. The burial shroud around my heart unwinds, allowing the dying parts of my heart to resurrect. Breathing in "sh-kahch," I find a deeper repose in what preceded my small self: my soul. A revived, living, breathing small self begins to sprout from this new earth.

CHAPTER TWENTY-NINE

Bad Rep or Sparkling Profile

Key Words: b'neynasha, pherash, shaphira

*When you are drawn to this day, feel your heart standing free,
even in the middle of other people's opinions about you.*

In Yeshua's time people would have found it inconceivable that one
would be concerned with what a person halfway across the world
thought of them, either positively or negatively. Everything about reputation in those times arose either within a family, a relatively close community, or in the eyes of religious or political officials. Today we see how
worldwide communication can have pluses and minuses. It connects us
with many more people to share a larger community but also imports
all of the harmful, and ultimately illusory, features of most contemporary human communities—nationalism, racism, sexism, to name a few.

Yeshua recognized that it's very easy to see another in the clouded
mirror of our own heart, which was his way of talking about what we
call "projection." Likewise, it's equally easy to be seduced by the glitter
that adheres to our small self when we project a false image designed
to impress others. Basic human stuff. He tackles some of this in Luke's
Beatitudes, where he reframes for his listeners a bad reputation and a
sparkling one:

*"It can be blessedly ripening, just the right thing to discover your
true purpose . . .*

When your good name gets tossed about, shut out, carried here and there as if it were a waste of time to mention you . . .

All because someone (or some part of you) misviews the 'you' trying to fulfill its divine image, living according to its real purpose.

Likewise you can be cut off from blessed timing with your soul when people say only light, bright, and beautiful things about you . . .

When they look only at the outside of the glass and reflect back its surface . . .

*When there is no one around you who has the first inkling of how to speak the truth."**

Roots and Branches

All this, Yeshua says, takes place "within, before, and in front of our temporary humanity," *b'neynasha* (not translated in the KJV). We experience these things because we live individual lives with unique opportunities to experience the greater support of our soul, *ruha*. He underlines this when he talks about "for the son of man's sake," *helaph bar d'nasha*, literally because we are a child of humanity. (*Bar d'nasha* is not a title or honorific in Aramaic; see RAJ.) "Separate" is the Aramaic *pherash*, to disperse or hunt, as well as to mishear someone. "Well," in "speaking well," is a form of *shaphira*, something bright and sparkling on the surface. (See RAJ for more on this one too.)

Message for Today

Probably never before in human history has our consciousness felt so isolated and separate, as well as so entangled with the opinions of others whom we will likely never meet in person. To touch base with

---

* Luke 6:22, 26: "Blessed are ye, when men shall hate you, and when they shall separate you from their company, and shall reproach you, and cast out your name as evil, for the son of man's sake. Woe unto you, when all men shall speak well of you! for so did their fathers to the false prophets."

an "authentic self," our soul, becomes ever more difficult. Our individual human tendency to believe our own publicity has never been greater. As Yeshua points out, we can become so veiled by the flattery of others that we can no longer look honestly into the mirror of our own hearts and find a true reflection.

Perhaps now is a ripe time to cast aside all self-images, both negative and positive, at least for this moment, and bathe in the light and love of our soul's embrace. We may consciously play a certain game due to being part of the game of life, but we still need to remain alert to our soul's voice. John's Gospel reports that Jesus didn't entrust his *naphsha* to the opinion of others because he knew how rapidly those opinions could change and how forgetful human beings could be (John 2:24, RAJ).

CONTEMPLATION

Breathing an easy, natural breath in the heart, I open to receive and absorb all of the love and life that my soul is waiting to send me. Breathing the word "b-nay-nah-sha," I feel at the same time the depth of my human self, waiting to receive all these gifts.

Breathing in "pher-ash" and out "shaphira," I feel the swirl of distorted opinions of others being breathed away.

I can live happily and ripely—above, beyond, underneath, and even in the middle of the projections of others—and of myself.

CHAPTER THIRTY

An Eyeful of Sun

Key Words: ayna, peshiyta, nuhra

When you are guided or drawn to this day, take the opportunity to release past sights, sounds, and memories from your inner eye and feel a fresh spring of life energy gushing up. What if only now existed?

Much has been written (and streamed) over the past decade or so about "being in the now." So much that it's become a cliché and an abstract thought rather than a realization. Yeshua offers a deep, embodied meditation on the reality of it:

"The eye is the lamp that enlightens your flesh (otherwise just a corpse), allowing you to perceive things around and within you. It's also a spring receiving and sharing life-giving energy. When that spring is not stopped up and the eye is free, your corpse is only light, all awareness, pure consciousness."*

Roots and Branches

The first word translated "light" in the KJV is actually a container for the light, *shraga*—an enclosure that allows the light of guidance and right direction for the moment (ShR) to grow or expand (GA). The Aramaic

---

* Matt. 6:22: "The light of the body is the eye: if therefore thine eye be single, thy whole body shall be full of light."

word for light, used at the end of the saying, is *nuhra*, which is also "knowing," "perceiving," and "consciousness" (8). The word translated "body" is a form of *pegra*, corpse, a form without living breath or the light of consciousness (17). The "eye" is *ayna*, also a "spring" or "source," not only the physical eye. The eye (single) here stands for all of the senses as they help us conceive and perceive things or ideas in time and space.

Message for Today

If our bodies are really vehicles for the light of consciousness, then who is really the perceiver? Quantum physics has developed the notion of a field of "indeterminacy" from which particles are temporarily collapsed into time and space when or if someone is there to perceive the newly appearing stuff. But who is perceiving all of us perceivers? Who is the ultimate doer? This question has occupied human beings for millennia. But is the question one that can be answered in words or concepts, which are just more stuff (albeit mental)? Yeshua directs us back to our own experience and invites us to clear our "eye," allowing it to be simple and unencumbered with memories of the past, whether visual, mental, or emotional. Our senses can receive but also give light. Do we make use of the first ability but not the second? Yeshua repeatedly invites us to experience the Source of life and possibility arising every moment through our awareness, rather than mistake our outer perceptions for the only reality. Could we see the light within all of nature?

Perhaps life is calling you now to drop your memories of the past and your ideas of everything that seems to limit you, your family, or your community. Can you simply hold all these "eye-veils" as temporary and unnecessary for seeing and feeling clearly now. It can all begin with a contemplation as simple as the following one.

CONTEMPLATION

I begin using Aramaic words breathed in and around the heart. (And yes, these too are more "stuff," but like a natural herb, the substance will dissolve into pure experience, leaving no harmful residue.)

Breathing "shra-gah," I feel my flesh as a container to allow the light of consciousness to shine through me, revealing a world shared with other human beings as well as—and this is important—unique to me. A world created anew.

I sense my eyes and seeing, including my inner sight. I breathe in "ay-nah" (eye, senses) and breathe out "pesh-ee-tah" (freed of baggage, cleared of clouds). As I breathe out, I release, breath by breath, the certainty that what I saw, felt, and perceived in the past was anything more than a blip, an evaporating drop in the flow of time. (This is a sobering contemplation, but if life has led you to this day, it might be time to do this deep releasing.) I continue with the other senses in the same way.

Then (or another time), I simply breathe the word "nuh-rah"—light, knowing, experiencing. This clear light, unclouded, is nothing other than the flow of life and love that created the cosmos, as well as me and my perception of it. I feel the meeting place of all my senses, the light appears there, too. The sun comes out, freeing me. I release all words and simply shine.

CHAPTER THIRTY-ONE

Wake-up Call:
Being Empty, Being Full

Key Words: hasha, khaphna, sab`a

> *When you are drawn here, become aware today of any tendency*
> *to hold onto feeling either empty or full. Could it be possible for*
> *both states to flow freely through you?*

One of the things that seems most out of joint with modern life is our tendency to either hold onto things too long or release them too quickly. For instance, Western economics is driven by the need to constantly create and consume more products, leading to more waste. An economy that is not growing is seen as not healthy. Couldn't we see growth and decline, or consumption and conservation, as polarities united by a balance point in the middle?

Yeshua promotes a change in course beginning with our own inner "economy," starting with being empty and full. In the Beatitudes in Luke, he urgently warns us to wake up to both the limited moments we have in the flesh as well as the fact that, in time and space, one state naturally changes into another. Here are two of his sayings that aim to bring us back into balance:

> "Ripening into blessing now are you who feel empty but still feel
> full. . . . Warnings now to any of you holding onto feeling full;
> you are really always feeling empty."*

---

* Luke 6:21, 25: "Blessed are ye that hunger now: for ye shall be filled. Woe unto you that are full! for ye shall hunger."

Roots and Branches

The key Aramaic word here is *hasha*, which means not only "now" but tells Yeshua's audience to "Wake up now, this moment!" Here he addresses those who know real hunger (*khaphneyn*) and at the same time are able to feel full (*saba*) due to a connection to their *ruha*-soul through the heart (12). We saw a different form of the second word in the fourth line of Yeshua's prayer (7). When he comes to the "woe" part, he issues a "warning," the Aramaic word *wai*, to those who hold onto being full (a different form of *saba*). This obsession reveals that they are always feeling empty (a different form of *khaphneyn*). What's not clear in the usual translation is that all this can be happening in any particular moment, *hasha*, not in an if-then or present-future way of looking at life (see also RAJ).

Message for Today

Our potential to feel either full or empty, either hungry or satiated, all exist together. Outer personal circumstances can change quickly. If we stay in the middle, our *leba*-heart can embrace both sides of the seesaw. On the community level, we can see that if one group always holds onto being full, this enforces a state of outer emptiness on another group. This is a big flag—*wai*—a warning that something is massively out of balance, says Yeshua. No collective heart. Understandably, religious-political officials of his time found this teaching very upsetting.

Perhaps life is calling us to simply be in a *hasha* moment, to wake up to our tendency to hold onto either fullness or emptiness, including keeping ourselves either too busy or not engaged enough in life. Whatever unripeness goes on around us, Yeshua advises us to first issue a warning bell on the breath to our own *naphsha* before we undertake what our *ruha* shows us we can do about outer injustice.

CONTEMPLATION

I breathe first the word "hah-shah" easily and naturally in and around my heart. Then I open my heart more, beyond my personal condition, to the source of love and light streaming around me from my soul. Can I feel that I am in *ruha*, rather than it being in me? And that this soul is much larger—it holds the potential for everything I need in life if I can regard the material and thought-stuff of life as temporary, yet important, appearances.

From a soul's eye view, I call the various "voices" of my *naphsha* together, as though around a common table. I breathe the word "kahf-neyn," hunger, and notice which part of my personal self responds. Am I always hungering for more experiences, more projects, more, more? After some time, I drop in the word "sah-bah," and notice again, my tendency to want to remain full. I continue to embrace the self from the larger viewpoint of heart and soul. Holding both words and feelings together, first out-breath ("kahf-neyn") then in-breath ("sah-bah"), I feel what food my soul is offering me right now, *hasha*.

CHAPTER THIRTY-TWO

Rejoice, Feel Free:
Let Your Heart Choose Today

Key Words: hadaw, rwaz, agarah

*When you are guided here, accept the opportunity to allow
your deepest heart, the doorway to your soul, to make your
choices today. The whole day is free.*

Today most of us value individual human freedom as the greatest good.
But what kind of freedom is it really? A freedom to make the limited
choices that a view of reality only grounded in material stuff and past
concepts affords us? Or that leads us to view our individual self, the
naphsha, as the greatest good? Even from the viewpoint of scientistic
humanism, this has created an epidemic of unhappiness and depres-
sion, as well as the precarious exploitation and destruction of nature.
Isn't there an option to live life both here and now, and everywhere all
the time, so in both our *naphsha* and *ruha*?

Yeshua points out that being misunderstood, projected upon,
and driven out of our comfort zone is the consequence—in time
and space—of following the inner voice of our soul (29, 35). Then he
encourages us:

*"From the point of now, feel joy and guidance, the abundance of
'what's just enough.'*

Become the leading shoot of a new plant of Reality's growth,

spreading to connect the life of your soul with the power within
all souls

who are traveling the prophetic caravan in front of and behind
you."*

Roots and Branches

"Rejoice" is the key word *hadaw*, from a root pointing to the joy one feels
when following the voice of the soul's guidance, not becoming lost in all
the possible choices that come to the self via the thoughts cluttering the
surface of our hearts (17). The word also implies that, while there seems
to be outer limitation in following the *ruha* in any moment, that limitation leads to the greatest sense of freedom, inside and out. There is only
one choice in each moment from the soul's point of view, so we become
free. Likewise, "exceedingly glad" is a form of *rwaz,* which really means
becoming thin, shedding whatever portion of our self-image, held by the
naphsha, prevents us from hearing this voice of guidance. These veils
especially appear as memories and stories about our past. The "reward"
is a form of the word *agarah*: the image of a large tree or plant growing
and expanding from a central root. That root is our soul, *ruha*. Yeshua
uses a parallel "vine and branches" image in John 15:5 (see RAJ).

Message for Today

What if we could truly understand that, in relation to the ultimate
source of happiness, holding less on the outside—less stuff either physically, mentally, or emotionally—allows us to travel more lightly in the
caravan of life? As Yeshua mentions, life cooperates whenever changes
in our outer circumstances alert us of the need to shed some of our
naphsha's baggage. Shedding such baggage is the *reason* many people go
on personal retreats (see appendices).

---

* Matt. 5:12: "Rejoice, and be exceeding glad: for great *is* your reward in heaven:
for so persecuted they the prophets which were before you."

Nearly forty-five years ago, I went on a personal retreat and had obtained a version of the words to the Aramaic Prayer of Jesus (the Lord's Prayer). After preparation, long silence, and many days in, I began to intone the first words of the prayer on one note. I found my body beginning to sway and move on its own, and I heard melodies, which continued as I chanted through the whole first four lines. Then I received a message that this was meant to be shared. When I returned home, I was tempted to forget about the whole thing but felt in my heart that I needed to at least try. A few people who were interested in this strange language began to gather around. Five years later, I met Dr. Matthew Fox, who hired me for his university institute in California, where I began to teach the prayer, its chants, and movements for his students. He helped me with publishing my first book a few years later.

CONTEMPLATION

Breathing "hah-daw" on my in- and out-breath, I center again in the heart. Can I open to the source of love, life, and light—above, underneath, and all around me? Can I feel my connection with this source high above me and then flowing with love and life energy down through my whole body all the way to the center of the earth? Guidance and joy are there, too.

My heart is the balance point between being expanded in the unseen world and fully earthed in this one. Can I feel myself rooted in the unlimited soul-force that includes both, able to feel joy right now? If so, then I am ready to hear the answer to the question: What is really mine to do next?

CHAPTER THIRTY-THREE

Shining City on a Mountain of Fire

Key Words: enuwn, nuhre d'alma

When you are drawn to this day, take the opportunity to change your starting place—from being a limited self in a body to an unlimited consciousness using some "best before" flesh for a while.

If we could take our next breath from the preceding feeling, it can change our whole experience of life. It sounds easy, but how do we feel this "unlimited" soul, which Yeshua calls *ruha*? If we tune into the channel that opens to love, light, or life energy all around us, we are halfway there. We can also tune in through our senses—seeing, smelling, touching, tasting, hearing—and then rediscover, at their meeting place, a surprise: a doorway opening through Sacred Sense (Holy Wisdom) to our soul.

Yeshua uses several metaphors in the Sermon on the Mount, pointing us in the right direction, including:

"You are Becoming itself—light and perception moving to, through, into, and from all the worlds around you. Your consciousness is like a community of give-and-take, a city sitting on a mountain of fire that cannot be hidden, compressed, or overshadowed."*

---

* Matt. 5:14: "Ye are the light of the world. A city that is set on a hill cannot be hid."

Roots and Branches

The words translated "you are" (usually overlooked) are the Aramaic *antuwn anwun*—not a fixed state of being, but a process in which an individual self (*ina* or here as *an*) appears and generates "descendants"— memories, experiences, and thoughts (*nw* from *hw*). Through having a *naphsha*-self, we have experiences that are meant to be the "light," *nuhre* (including all of the senses) that fill the world. This is how the world as we perceive it arises, individually and collectively. It is an appearance generated by *nuhra*, the knowing of the Knower. Yeshua compares the community of multiple feelings and sense impressions reacting within us and with each other to a city of residents, giving and receiving, all sitting on a mountain formed of fire (*d'al tuwra*). It cannot be "hidden" (*l'meshka*): overshadowed, compressed, or contracted. We appear as what we are, even if we think we are "hiding out." "World" is *alma*, not the earth, but all the worlds and levels of form (24).

Message for Today

Far from being a statement commissioning people to go out and propagate a doctrine of beliefs, this very deep statement points to the nature of our consciousness. This is not to say that what we perceive around us doesn't exist. For instance, a rainbow is no less real because we know it is not material. Yet Yeshua is coaxing his listeners to remember where our individual feelings, thoughts, and perceptions come from, as well as what they are intended for: to penetrate the worlds of form, as well as unseen worlds, with the light of consciousness, that is, with light, life, and love.

Perhaps life is asking you right now to change the place from which you begin to meditate, pray, engage in therapy, or do anything. Do you find yourself running around in circles, like a hamster in a wheel? If so, you can absolutely get off the wheel, says Yeshua. We all have this capability within us, baked in from when our soul gave birth to our form. We don't need to wait for years to change this starting place or for some perfect teacher or self-help guide to rescue us. We can begin now.

CONTEMPLATION

Settling comfortably, I bring the rhythm of my breathing together with the subtle feeling of my heartbeat, perhaps by placing one hand very lightly over my heart. Then I add in the word "an-woon," (becoming) on the in-breath and on the out-breath "nooh-ray d' al-mah" (light and perception of all levels and worlds). This is a direct connection to my deepest, highest, most intuitive source. I dive through my heart into the soul, the Big Breath that connects me to everything around me, including the angelic world.

After some minutes, I release these words and simply breathe, feeling my heart as a gathering place for the impressions received through all my senses. All together. In the center of this circle: light. Light illuminates and clarifies both my individual life as well as the perception of the world around me.

I repeat this meditation as needed until I can begin and end each day from this mountain of fire and light. Then I punctuate more of my day with "light moments" until it becomes natural—my "first nature" rather than my second.

CHAPTER THIRTY-FOUR

Wake-up Call:
Tears and Laughter

Key Words: hasha, beka, gehek

> *When you are drawn to this day, become aware of any ten-*
> *dency to force a laugh or hold onto tears longer than feels*
> *natural. Can you allow both to flow freely and spontaneously*
> *through you?*

Already in his time Yeshua recognized our human tendency to ride on the surface of life rather than plumb its depths toward the Source from which everything arises. Today we talk about forced hilarity or a person shedding "crocodile tears" (perhaps doing an injustice to crocodiles). It seems, however, that at least in Western culture a person's ability to recognize when another is really being sincere in their expression of emotion has diminished, as each person has become more enclosed within their own small self-*naphsha*. We are living in an increasingly selfie-selfish world. Instead of genuine empathy, we often see someone express a mock emotion that does not really empathize with the person in need but rather focuses on themselves and how they appear.

Just as he does about feeling full and empty (31), Yeshua offers a simple way to test whether we are being genuinely ripe (*tubw*), in the moment: Do we find ourselves compulsively veering away from one state and toward another? In this one Yeshua reframes both tears and laughter:

> *"You are ripening now when you feel wrung out like a sponge, freely flowing tears inviting you to enter the larger, lighter, life-dance of your soul.*
>
> *"Warning: You are in danger now when your laughter becomes hollow, outer hilarity covering up your soul's voice."**

Roots and Branches

As we've seen, Luke's Beatitudes focus on being aware now (*hasha*), directly and personally, of what our soul is trying to tell us. To shock the small self into awareness, Yeshua shows how an unpleasant state can lead to a happiness that is always "on time" (*tubwaykhun*, ripe are *you*), and how a pleasant state compulsively grasped can provide a warning bell (the Aramaic *wai*, warning, usually translated "woe"). "Weep" is a form of *beka*, being wrung out like a sponge. "Laugh" is a form of *gehek*, also meaning "to being carried freely," "laughing," or "dancing."

Message for Today

We tend to want to make a set of axioms to live by so we can go on autopilot, our hands off the steering wheel. Yeshua uses language that aims to shake us awake, to touch the deep core of our self, and to open us again to the soul's voice. He would like us to be aware of a tendency to seek out either negative or positive experiences for what their temporary payoff might be. If we continually recalibrate to our soul, then we will have enough of both in our lives (38).

---

* Luke 6:21, 25: "Blessed are ye that weep now: for ye shall laugh. Woe unto you that laugh now! for ye shall mourn and weep."

Perhaps now is a ripe time to have another *hasha* moment, a reality check during the course of today—this one on our tendency to hold onto a particular emotion or expression of it simply because it's easier or more familiar. For Yeshua, life in time and space is by nature limited and changing, while the *ruha*-soul is free. As he says in the Gospel of Thomas: "If the flesh comes into being because of breath and soul, that is a marvel, but if breath and soul come into being because of the flesh, that is a marvel of marvels. Yet I marvel at how this great wealth has come to dwell in this poverty" (Saying 29).

CONTEMPLATION

Breathing "hah-sha" in and around the heart, I make an intention to enter the present moment, connecting with the source of love, light, and life always present when I enter the soul's happiness.

Then I call a circle of my inner self, the naphsha's community of voices or impressions. I breathe with the word "bey-ka." Are there genuine tears that want to be shed now? And after a while I breathe with "gehek." Is there genuine laughter that wants to be felt now? Can I breathe with and hold both words, both feelings, together in the heart? I notice how, throughout my life's changes, both have flowed best when they have flowed naturally—"tubwaykhun!"

CHAPTER THIRTY-FIVE

Moving On—For Inner Honesty and Outer Justice

Key Words: redep, khenuta, malkuta dashmaya

When you are drawn to this day, take the opportunity to consider whether you need to move out of either your "outer house"—your situation in life—or your "inner house"—your cherished, but overly limited ideas, ideals, and concepts.

Popular Western culture is very careful these days not to disturb its citizens' sense of settled comfort—particularly emotionally and mentally—hence the proliferation of trigger warnings. For Yeshua, however, being moved out of and beyond our usual comfort zone was often the sign that we were following the voice of soul-*ruha*, heard in our deepest heart. How can we discover this deeper heart if the flotsam and jetsam of thoughts and emotions on its surface are never sieved away? Toward the end of the Beatitudes in Matthew, Yeshua comments that, for becoming a channel for the soul's peace, one can expect to be dislocated:

> *"Tuning to ripeness are those who, for the sake of inner honesty and outer justice, are pushed through the boundaries temporarily set by others or their own self. They are entering the larger life shining around them and being renewed by its vision and power."**

---

* Matt. 5:10: "Blessed are they which are persecuted for righteousness' sake: for theirs is the kingdom of heaven."

Roots and Branches

"Persecuted" is a form of the Aramaic *redep*: pushing through or toward something, bursting out of the earth like a spring of water. "Righteousness" is a word we saw earlier (12), *khenuta*, a balance of inner honesty and outer justice—at the minimum acting in accordance with the way one would like to be treated. Both "blessed" (*tubwhayhun*) and "kingdom of heaven" (*malkuta dashmaya*) also appeared in the first Beatitude (2): a ripeness found in conscious presence of the moment, leading to an experience of the vision and power that created the cosmos. The Beatitude in Matthew that follows this one includes not only being "pushed beyond" but also being envied, conspired against, defamed, and projected upon (similar to what appears in Luke, see 29, or RAJ, chapter 3).

Message for Today

The journey of breakthrough that begins with finding our home in the breath (2) winds through many stages. Yeshua now includes dealing with the most problematic aspects of our lives with others. While the desire to "stay ripe" could lead us to disengage from most interactions with people, Yeshua warns against this in his prayer (27). Likewise, he warns us to be beware of our desire to blame others and ignore the voice of our deep heart. Instead, we need to demand honesty from ourselves with clear, calm reflection on the inner state of our *naphsha*. We can find balance and happiness only in our deepest heart's connection to the Big Breath and Heart, which opens a channel to our soul.

Perhaps life is calling you to review recent events that have led you to feel you need to move beyond either an outer structure of community or family, or an inner "house" constructed of your own collection of past habits, thoughts, memories, and even ideals. You can be grateful for what helped you to this point but still affirm that the time has come to relocate your activities and thoughts closer to your soul's real desire in the name of *khenuta*. As Yeshua says in the Gospel of Thomas (42), "Become passers-through."[†]

---

† Often poorly translated as "Be passersby."

CONTEMPLATION

I begin again breathing with the feeling of "tooh-bway-hoon" in and around my heart, allowing the word to rise and fall in a relaxed way.

Then I bring in any feeling of being pushed beyond, being finished with a certain phase of my life, or shedding an old skin that restricts me. With this feeling in the mirror of my heart, I breathe out the sound "reh-dehp," going further, flowing out, and I breathe in feeling "khe-noo-tah," honesty and justice. As I breathe out, I release what I am leaving behind, and as I breathe in, I face a more free, honest future, one centered in my soul's purpose.

When it's time, I open and relax into feeling the larger community awaiting me—other possibilities, people, and communities. They are all part of "mal-koo-tah dash-may-ah," and as I breathe with these words, I can now see, sense, and feel this much larger world opening around me.

CHAPTER THIRTY-SIX

Finding the Rhythm
of Rapport

Key Words: ruha, ahebw, abedu

*When you are drawn to this day, find yourself in the very center
of your heart, now able to sense the rhythm of breath matching
that of a problematic person or situation you are facing. Then
lovingly find and change this rhythm in yourself.*

Dealing with challenging people and situations usually requires much
patience. This means stopping our sense of time passing and entering
the *now* of our deepest heart, its window open to our Big Breath–connected soul, *ruha*. And what then? Yeshua's own method seems to have
been to first go to that timeless place and then reenter one's breathing
in a conscious way, sensing how the rhythm of a more free and flexible
breath can enter and permeate what we are finding problematic. Can I
sense this other rhythm in myself? How is this out of step with my own
usual one? This does not require any special "extra-sensory" abilities,
because as human beings we all can sense a "good" or "bad atmosphere"
in a room when we enter it. At the end of his Beatitudes in Luke, Yeshua
concludes:

*"Find the patient, loving breath and action that match the rhythm
of the one whose breath and rhythm don't harmonize with your
own. Then serve them a change-up: in return for the projection*

> *of their own self-loathing onto you, offer them a serving of light,*
> *bright, and beautiful praise, inside and out."**

Roots and Branches

"Love" here is a form of *ahebw*, a patient, slowly growing, give-and-take love that can entrain and harmonize with anyone, including a person "out of rhythm" with you, *b^celdbabayka*, translated "enemy" in the KJV. So any situation in which one feels disharmony reflects a disharmony in our own breath. The "hate" that we feel coming toward us, *sane'*, means a coloring, like colored glasses that the person wears to see us (or with which we see ourselves). When this happens, Yeshua advises us to do something they're not expecting: we shine more brightly (*shaphiry*, translated "good"), offering the praise or acknowledgment the other's *naphsha*-self really wants subconsciously.

Message for Today

At first glance, Yeshua's advice seems at least counterintuitive if not somewhat hypocritical. We need to remember that in the Beatitude sayings just prior to this, he asks us repeatedly to return to the voice of our soul before we do anything. In this view, our small self, our individual sense of "me," is an instrument for the soul to make life choices that uncover wisdom and share love. First, we need to be honest with ourselves about where we're coming from. Then we can consider our own preferences equally with those of another viewed through the soul's light of patience. This begins with the barest tolerance and progresses gradually to respect, and perhaps friendship (3). This doesn't mean we don't see a person or situation clearly. Yet so that we do not continue to participate in their out-of-time unripeness in relation to us, we need to

---

* Luke 6:27: "Love your enemies, do good to them which hate you."

make sure we don't harbor resonances of it in ourselves. If we find these, we have full freedom and power to release them.

Yes, tough medicine. This is Yeshua's "advanced course" in ripeness. Perhaps life is calling you to stop for a moment, disengage from a situation, and then enter the timeless dimension of our *ruha*. If we only look at the outer side of a situation, we will never perceive or feel the bigger picture through the eyes of our deeper heart.

CONTEMPLATION

Breathing an easy, natural breath in and around the heart, I again go through this doorway of love and life energy into a time and space where everything I need is already present. I breathe in and out with the sounds "roo-hah" or "roo-hah d'qood-shah (18)."

First, I absorb all of the loving energy (breathing "ah-heb") I could wish for. It's all around me—beneath me in the center of the earth and above me as far as I can sense and feel. Then I bring into my heart mirror the image of a person with whom I am having problems (or a part of my self). Can I sense a breathing connection to them? Could I stay connected to that Big Breath of my soul? I begin to shine from the deepest place inside while breathing "sha-phir," irradiating any of my own self-projections as well as those of any person or situation with which I'm entangled. I am not who the other thinks I am, nor who I think I am.

CHAPTER THIRTY-SEVEN

A Lamp Kindled in Your Flesh

Key Words: shraga, manhar

When you are drawn to this day, accept the opportunities that life is presenting for you to embody your soul's light more fully.

When people talk to me about their spiritual path, one of the main goals I hear is that they want to embody their devotional life, prayer, or practice and make it useful in everyday life. These are worthy intentions, although I find that people often want to build up this experience in small increments rather than all at once, like the prayer of the 4th century CE Augustine of Hippo: "Lord, make me pure, but not yet!"

Yeshua reminds us that buried within us, built in from our birth, we can find a light that offers the ability to use our senses clearly. It's seeded in every person. Otherwise, we would not even be able to perceive any world around or within us, as well as share the same outer world with all other human beings. Following an earlier saying (33), he compares our human consciousness to a lamp:

> *"No one kindles a lamp and places it under a measuring cup, doling out bits here and there. They place it on a lamp stand so that its fire and light spread everywhere."**

---

* Matt. 5:15: "Neither do they light a candle, and put it under a bushel, but on a candlestick; and it giveth light unto all that are in the house."

Roots and Branches

What's translated here as "candle" is the Aramaic *shraga*, really a lamp or any enclosure that allows light to radiate (30). The word for "light" is a form of *manhar*, to kindle a lamp, itself a form of *nuhra*, but here meaning to ignite fire from a substance. The word usually translated "bushel" is *sa'ta*, any sort of container for measuring. The "candlestick" is *mnarta*, based on the word for "kindle," here meaning any form of firelight that allows its light to grow and spread. "House" is *bayta*, including our flesh, our community, and our "inner house" of thoughts and ideals.

Message for Today

From long before the time of Yeshua, the ancients viewed everything as containing fire, which was only waiting for the proper kindling to spark it into heat and light. The human being was the same. In Yeshua's time a lamp used oil to produce fire and light. In our lifetime, what gets gradually consumed as fuel is our inner oil, our *naphsha* and its enfleshed life energy. Yeshua uses a similar image in his parable of the women waiting for a bridal party, some of whom had oil to burn, some not (see RAJ, chapter 5).

Our lives here in time and space are a precious opportunity to kindle the fire and light within us, which arises from another source, the *nuhra* of *Alaha*. This light comes from an unlimited source and does not consume our enfleshed life energy. Instead it reinvigorates it. We can find this light all around us viewed in the depths of nature as well as other people in the world. Another way Yeshua puts this is: connect individual self, *naphsha*, to its source, *ruha*, I-I, and you will then find and become the "light of the world," since every person's real light, life, love, and soul are connected to everyone and everything else (33).

Perhaps life is calling you to consider how you are using the oil of your life. Are you using it to shine without holding back, to hide the light, or to measure it out in small bits here and there? Yeshua recommends the first choice. Light is light. Let it shine throughout your whole inner and outer house. Then do what you do.

CONTEMPLATION

Breathing again in and around the heart, I connect to the light, feeling the word "nooh-rah" riding on my breath, taking me deeper and deeper into a connection with the love, light, and life energy all around me. I don't need any special method or permission to feel this. It's what is creating my embodied human self and the world right now.

Then I breathe in feeling the word "man-har" (kindle) and breathe out feeling "shrah-gah" (lamp). Can I feel that light and heat in my heart, including my individual passion and love? That larger, warmer light is already here, just waiting to be kindled. The spark: my sincere intention to connect with its Source all around me and in the unseen world.

Sometimes I bring this combination of words into my heart as I'm walking in nature where I will not feel restricted. Light and life spread all around me.

CHAPTER THIRTY-EIGHT

Tomorrow Means Things Depart

Key Words: sapheq, yawma

*When or if you are guided to this day, enjoy the opportunity
to let go of yesterday and everything that caused you to forget
that you are really an unlimited ruha, a Big Breath, temporarily living in a small breath, your naphsha.*

The more we human beings control our environment (or believe we do), the more apt we are to fall prey to a central illusion, from Yeshua's point of view: that we can in any way control our past and future. The only thing we can control is the way we view the things, events, and concepts we've already experienced and how we choose to feel and act in the future. Yeshua points this out in an often misunderstood saying in the Gospels. An Aramaic view offers a more subtle view, one that is a meditation in itself:

Don't torture yourself standing watch over things, accomplishments, or states of mind you still want to possess tomorrow. It doesn't work that way. Tomorrow means things depart.

Time and the elements wash them away just as they came, with abundance, as the future stands by watching.

Each day completes itself with its own share of unripeness.

Every illumination carries enough inappropriate action without carrying any forward.*

Roots and Branches

Key here are the words for "taking thought," which really mean to try to hold onto and make fixed (*hakhiyl*) a flow of material phenomena and linked thoughts (*tsbphuwn*), a stream that can never be fixed or limited. What we perceive and think pass away (or should in their natural state). If we continually label them positive, negative, pleasing, or displeasing, they can become idols or obsessions that possess us. "Tomorrow" is *mchar*, from roots meaning what passes away into light. "Sufficient" is *sapheq*, whatever completes a process or activity. "Day" (*yauma*) is also related to light, a period or temporary "particle" of the wave of time perceived while I have a flesh and "particle-self" (11). What completes each illuminated period for us, each day, each bundle of impressions and phenomena, is what is not ripe, *bisha*, for the next moment (27). What we may experience as "time out of joint" is due to the way we hold onto memories of the past or expectations of what we believe should happen in the future.

Message for Today

According to Yeshua, it's best to let bits of time and the components of things and thoughts wash away each day, rather than misuse our memory to stand watch over whatever we feel didn't go right, or even what did. Why build more beautiful or imposing bars around the cage of our *naphsha*, the small breath-self? Likewise, Yeshua recommends not "standing watch" over what might happen tomorrow because whatever

---

* Matt. 6:34: "Take therefore no thought for the morrow: for the morrow shall take thought for the things of itself. Sufficient unto the day is the evil thereof." See DW for full Aramaic.

the next moment presents should be as free as possible of the previous moment.

Perhaps life is offering you the opportunity to release near and dear impressions of what you believe went wrong in the past, things you continually chew over that end up chewing you. Or even to challenge the inner house of beliefs in which you found a life that is comfortable but ultimately limiting and unfulfilling. These inner houses can entrap us even more than our perceived psychological foibles. In short, they don't allow our Big Breath, *ruha*, to breathe through us and create a renewing, truly free life.

CONTEMPLATION

I return to breathing an easy, natural breath, first feeling my heart area, then expanding to feel the larger Breath of Life, *ruha d'qud-sha*, surrounding me. The breath in my physical lungs arises from this Big Breath. It sends the love and gratitude that surrounds me and provides my life energy.

As added support, I breathe in and out feeling two words in Yeshua's saying: breathing in "sah-feq," completing, and breathing out "yaw-mah," this day. This illuminated moment is completing itself, bringing everything to fruition that the day requires, either ripe or unripe. Placing my forehead on the floor or earth—and breathing while feeling my heart above my head—helps me release more.

As I am letting go of memories of the past day, I release expectations of tomorrow. The Big Breath comes through, with love, light, and life, and helps me witness the opportunities arriving in the next moment.

CHAPTER THIRTY-NINE

Open Way or Hidden Way, Straight or Zigzag?

Key Words: hakima, hewata, yauna

When you are guided here, consider how open or hidden to be in a situation. Then take the opportunity to rest in between the two—in the deeper wisdom of the heart.

Today we are increasingly confronted with the question of how open or secretive we should be about what's going on in our lives. The prevalence of social media has made this issue very pressing. On one hand, we feel the natural human tendency to reach out and connect. Our *ruha*-soul is always in connection with *Alaha*, so connecting becomes part of what our *naphsha* always wants to do. Yet on the other hand, you may have also found, as I have, that it's sometimes wisest not to overshare about what one is doing or envisioning. This does not conflict with what Yeshua says about hiding our light under a measure, which is about our intention and radiance, not necessarily our outer actions (37).

In ancient Semitic languages, all of the words that can mean "to plan" also mean "to deceive oneself." As we explored yesterday, banking too much on our expectations of tomorrow leads ultimately to disappointment. At the same time, our contemporary culture places a great value (even if it's not always followed) on "being straight" about what one wants and expects from a relationship or job, for instance. How to square this seeming circle? Yeshua recommends we travel to a place between these alternatives before deciding whether to go straight or zigzag toward a goal:

> *Sometimes be subtle, like Holy Wisdom—*
> *follow her spiral way like a snake weaving back and forth,*
> *no movement the same as the last.*
> *Include all, exclude none, like Eve, the first Mother of us all.*
> *Sometimes feel Holy Wisdom's passion—*
> *fly straight to the Beloved like a dove*
> *moving all at once, clearly, obviously.*
> *Open your wings wholeheartedly, already at one with your goal.**

Roots and Branches

The key word here, usually translated simply "wisdom," is *Hakima*, the Aramaic name for Holy Wisdom in Yeshua's language. From its roots, the word points to a gathering of sense impressions deep inside in a center that "makes sense" of all the myriad of things we see, hear, smell, taste, and touch through our awareness. Who or what allows us to say, for example, "I see, smell . . . and so forth?" For ancient Semitic language speakers, this was the Sacred Sense behind and in the middle of our outwardly reaching, grasping senses.† The word for "snake" used by Jesus, *hewata*, also invokes *Hewa*, the first "life-giver," the biblical Eve. The word for "dove" is the Aramaic *yauna*. Both snakes and doves were associated in ancient Southwest Asia with Holy Wisdom.

Message for Today

Could we rest within all of our senses for a moment, feeling the center of them? Then immediately upon reentering our outer perception,

---

* Matt. 10:16: "Be ye therefore wise as serpents, and harmless as doves." See RAJ and DW for more on Holy Wisdom.

† For more on this, see my rendering of the Coptic text "Thunder, Perfect Mind" in DW.

could our *ruha*-soul choose a zigzag or straight way, a subtle or open way, depending on the situation? From the center of sensing, everything arises from this kindled light. Yeshua repeatedly counsels us that no one personal habit of privacy or openness might fit the next moment. He often spoke in parables. He also overturned the moneylenders' tables in the Jerusalem Temple.

Perhaps life is calling you away from a knee-jerk reaction to a situation. The "snake or dove" path asks that we first pause and allow Holy Wisdom to embrace us, opening a window in our heart between soul and self, *ruha* and *naphsha*. Again, part of Yeshua's "advanced course."

CONTEMPLATION

Breathing again in and around my heart, my eyes are half open. I breathe with the word "hah-kee-mah" and relax into a space that feels as though it's just behind the heart. Then I progressively become aware of my seeing, hearing, tasting, smelling, and sense of touch, one after the other. I then feel all of the senses together and "fall backward" into the place that unites them, the arms of Sacred Sense.

I may only remain there for a moment, but the more I relax and feel the heart, the more I return to this place, the easier it becomes. Rest. Renew. Re-View.

I breathe and begin to gaze through the heart with Hakima's eyes. Then as I review a situation in front of me, I breathe the word "hewata," the snake way, and notice the response in my heart feeling and breathing. I do the same for "yauna," the dove way. I compare. I do it all again or twice more, at a different moment, then act.

CHAPTER FORTY

Let Light Shine from the Beginning—of You!

Key Words: ninhar nuhrakhun, qadam b'neynasha

When you are drawn to this day, affirm your limitless ability to shine and unfold in works of love at just the right time and place.

Once I accept that I am not who I think I am . . .

That my "I" is connected through all human beings to what is always creating that "I," the Only "I" . . .

That my physical body is a "corpse" unless animated by a light and life energy that is beyond as well as within me . . .

That this breath-life energy ultimately comes from an unseen world, rather than as a result of rearranging individual elements in my body into ever-more complex forms . . .

That there is a larger Heart and larger Breath of which my own are a part—and have always been, from before birth to after death . . .

Then all I need to do is remember more and more, which as we saw (39) can be as simple as falling backward through my heart into the arms of Sacred Sense, Holy Wisdom, hearing her music through me. Yeshua comments:

"Allow the light and awareness within you to radiate from the first Beginning. Your whole human self then illuminates all people.

They sense and perceive the results in what you do—work, service, loving—all in the ripe moment. It's a song reminding them that a larger creating and parenting Source, seen and unseen, is nurturing every instant, unfolding a cosmos made of vibration and light."

Roots and Branches

We have seen most of the Aramaic words before. Forms of "light," *nuhra,* appear twice in the beginning ("let your light shine") as *ninhar nuhrakun.* Again, this is not only physical light but our ability to sense and perceive through our physical senses, as well as send light. "Before all men" is *qadam b'neynasha,* which means "from before, from the original forming" (*qadam*) that is within and among (*b'ney*) all human beings in their time-limited form (*nasha*). So not simply before in the sense of "in front of" people. "Good works" is a form of *abada,* work and service that proceed from love, and *thauba,* ripe, a form of *tubw,* in the right time and place. "See" is *nehzun,* again meaning also to be illuminated (14). "Glorify" is a form of *sheba,* the song of return and renewal that fills the cosmos (24).

Message for Today

After we reframe our usual way of looking at life, which only views things outwardly, the unity of inner and outer life, the seen and the unseen, comes as a profound relief. It is the real "non-dualism," not an abstract idea of it. Our hearts, light, life, and love are within the larger Heart, but not separate from what is around us. And especially not separate from why we're here: to make our own heart-filled choices and act upon them. As we human beings have become ever more aware of our individuality, *choice* is the unique gift

---

* Matt. 5:16: "Let your light so shine before men, that they may see your good works, and glorify your Father which is in heaven." For more, see RAJ, chapter 5.

to us in our time. Will we use this gift to become ever more selfish and selfie, or the opposite?

In the Gospel of Thomas, Yeshua's students ask him, "How will our end be?" He replies, "You are already looking for the end. Have you revealed to yourself the beginning? Look! The end will be where the beginning is. The one who is blessedly ripe will come to standing in the beginning. That one will know the end and will not taste death. The blessedly ripe are those who come into being from the Beginning, before they existed" (Saying 18, 19a).[†]

Perhaps life is calling you to abandon anger, aggravation, indifference, and boredom and to feel the profound life energy that comes from connecting your heart to *ruha*, your breath to the Holy Breath. You are already a part of all this. Then to hear the song of the cosmos and play your notes in the music.

CONTEMPLATION

Breathing in the heart, easily and naturally, I feel "nin-har" (shine) on the in-breath and "noo-rah-koon" on the out-breath.

Is it possible to feel the light from before my birth shining through me? What if I could? It's the same light from before the beginning of the cosmos. Can a sense of awe remind me that this light continues after my flesh returns to its elements and my soul continues its journey?

Such a light can do nothing less than shine and grow a new world of possibilities within and around me.

---

† See RAJ, chapter 8, for more resonances of Thomas in the Gospel of John.

Some General Retreat Advice

Over the past forty years, I have advised many who wished to use the Prayer of Jesus, Beatitudes, or other Aramaic Jesus sayings for personal retreats. In addition, I have taken many retreats in my spiritual life and can say that many of my real breakthrough experiences have occurred in a solo retreat atmosphere. Here are a few observations, which might prove helpful:

1. Being on retreat is about discovering a different, usually slower, rhythm of awareness than is usually possible in everyday life. Finding one's way into and back from these slightly or greatly altered states of awareness is something that becomes easier with practice. No amount of practice can command or induce states of grace or inspiration from *Alaha*. However, one can prepare oneself to receive them.

2. Using spiritual practice, chanting, breathing meditation, and body awareness practice on retreat eases entry into and exit from these various states of awareness. Painting, drawing, singing, and other various forms of art-as-meditation may provide a way to hear the voice of the *ruha*-soul more clearly. Using a structured model can act as a lens for this voice and help develop an inner sense of the beginning, middle, and end of a process. As you begin to discover doorways and passages in your own being, you may find you move from a more to a less structured retreat. After several retreats, as you find your own

retreat rhythm, you may notice that the difference between "sessions" and "breaks" becomes meaningless: it is just *being*, on retreat.

3. Preparing one's *naphsha*-self for grace to appear asks some effacement or softening of it. How willing am I to really receive an answer from my highest guidance, the voice of my *ruha*? How sincere does my voice sound when I say, "Let your heart's desire bring heaven and earth together in my life?" *Nehwey sebyanach aykanna d'bwashmaya aph b'arha.* The small self must cooperate, but the soul must lead. This balance can take years to discover, or it can be there in an instant. Only *khenuta*, full-hearted sincerity, is really required.

A Retreat with the Aramaic Prayer (the "Lord's Prayer")

The following are approximate transliterations (rendering into English characters) of the full Aramaic phrases. You can hear a pronunciation of the words as well as chanted melodies for them at my website (*https://abwoon.org*, "Aramaic Jesus Library" page) as well as on the "Prayers of the Cosmos" audio download. If you are new to this, choose to use only the key words in the corresponding chapter in this book, marked as (#) below.

The Aramaic Prayer of Jesus

The shape of the Prayer proceeds from One to one, soul to self, and back again.

1. **Abwun d'bashmaya:** *"O Birthing! Fathering-Mothering of the Cosmos, you are creating all that moves in light."* (5)

   I remember the source of Reality as the ever-creating energy and power behind the cosmos, as loving as a father and mother could ideally be. I give thanks for its role in my life to this point.

2. **Nethqadash shmakh:** *"Clear out heart space for the name-light-vibration of Abwun to focus our lives."* (6)

   I let go and clear space in my heart to hear the voice of inspiration. Breathing in the heart, I feel its surface as a mirror that becomes clearer and clearer with each breath, able to reflect the light-*shem* of *Abwun*.

3. **Teyte malkutakh:** *"Let arrive, with urgency, your voice of vision and agency, your I Can, here and now!"* (10)

In the space created, I allow the voice of the infinite to come through my heart. I allow whatever is received to settle and root itself in my heart.

4. **Nehwe sabyanach aykana d'bashmaya aph b'ar'ah:** *"Let the Breath of life create a new appearance of heart-desire in and through me, uniting heaven and earth, everywhen and here-now in my life."* (7)

I intend with full heart to align vision with purpose in life, asking for the deep willingness to make the vision of what is mine to do a practical reality.

5. **Habwlan lachma d'sunqanan yaomana:** *"Create for us the lachma we need for each and every moment of light that we have in this embodied life."* (11)

Hakima, or Holy Wisdom, the "mother" of *lachma* or practical understanding and food, welcomes me deeper into my *naphsha*. Breathing through my breath, she gathers its various "voices" together to be heard and fed. I offer these voices the breath and food of inspiration received in the previous line.

6. **Washboqlan khaubayn (wakhtahayn) aykana daph khnan shbwoqan l'khayyabayn:** *"Untangle the knots that compress my heart, making it rigid, unable to return to its natural flowing state. As I choose to release my end of a cord, the other end releases too."* (26)

I let go of whatever unripe impressions restrict the surface of my heart, including the impressions created by my self-*naphsha*. Sacred Breath, the source of my real "I," empowers this process.

7. **Wela tahlan l'nesyuna ela patsan min bisha:** *"Don't let us enter forgetfulness but free us from unripeness."* (27)

   I open and allow a channel of blessing to flow from my soul-*ruha* to my self-*naphsha.* I affirm an intention to walk a path between being too outer or too inner—with joy.

8. **Metol d'lakhe malkuta wahayla wateshbukhta l'ahlam almin ameyn:** *"In You, from You, lives all of the original vision and power, the life energy now, plus the melody of everything, a song returning to the heart of the cosmos, age to age, world to world, time to time, life to life. May I trust this ground of truth and live from here."* (24)

   I rededicate all vision, struggle, failure, and success to the Breathing Life of All, returning my song to the universal harmony.

At the end of the retreat, which is best done over eight days, you can experience again each line as a brief walking meditation, breathing with the phrase, or chant through the whole prayer. Then take some time to breathe in the heart and view your daily life with its challenges and opportunities, bringing the inspiration of the retreat to illuminate them.

A Retreat with the Aramaic Beatitudes

The following are approximate transliterations (rendering into English characters) of the full Aramaic phrases in the version in Matthew. You can hear a pronunciation of the words as well as chanted melodies at my website via the "Prayers of the Cosmos" audio download. If you are new to this, choose to use only the key words in the corresponding chapter in this book, marked as (#) below.

1. **Tubwayhun l'meskenaee b'rukh dilhounhie malkuta dash-maya:** *"Blessedly ripe, in the right moment, are those who rest in ruha as their first and last possession, their real home. To them is coming—at the same moment—the empowerment behind nature and all that is."* (2, also 9)

   I let go into the feeling of my breathing and the Sacred Breath of which it is a part. I honor this Big Breath and ask that it guide my retreat. I breathe into the two sides of my body fully and open a channel from the heart toward my highest guidance above me, which connects with the "table of Holy Wisdom" (the voices of my *naphsha*) down from the heart into my belly.

2. **Tubwayhun labwile d'hinnon netbayun:** *"Blessedly ripe are those who feel themselves falling into a bottomless pit of confusion and grief. By allowing their soul to catch them, they will find a new home that satisfies all desires and comforts them."* (21)

I allow suppressed or unfelt emotions to arise in my *naphsha*, including grief, confusion, anger, and denial. I breathe the key words in the meditation and/or use the gentle singing of the phrase to allow me to be present with these feelings and so begin to release them.

3. **Tubwayhun l'makikhe d'hinnon nertun ar^cah:** *"In ripeness are those who consciously soften what is too rigid within them. At the same time, they are receiving their natural inheritance of strength and healing from the gift of being part of nature's world, of being in a body in time and space."* (23)

   I soften and open to new strength and healing from nature. I walk and breathe with the power and beauty of the natural world, within and without.

4. **Tubwayhun layleyn d'khaphneyn wa tzheyn l'khenuta d'hinnon nesbuwn:** *"In happy ripeness are those who discover their real hunger and thirst—a life in which they are honest with themselves and deal justly with others. If they are hungry and thirsty enough, they will find around them a world in which this is possible.* (12)

   I dedicate my heart to *khenuta*, inner honesty and outer justice. *Hakima*, Holy Wisdom, gathers my whole *naphsha* to eat, drink, and be welcomed back home to connect with my *ruha*-soul.

5. **Tubwayhun lamrahmane dalayhun nehwun rahme:** *"In the right now-moment are those through whom a flow of deep love streams; they shall give birth to new, never-before-seen life in themselves and others."* (13)

   From this new communion of self and soul, I feel a connection with the Heart-Womb of the cosmos (*rahme*) and await the birth of a new "I am" within me.

6. **Tubwayhun layleyn dadkeyn b'lebhon d'hinnon nehzun l'alaha:** *"Full of joy, blissful in the Now, are those who find themselves*

feeling completely within their hearts; they shall be illuminated by signs of Reality wherever they look." (14)

I feel my heart as an altar upon which the inspiration and vision of *Alaha*—available to everyone—can appear. I walk with the feeling of this phrase or its key words, feeling the heart as a flaming light that illuminates my path ahead.

7. **Tubwayhun lᶜabwday shlama dabwnaw(hie) d'alaha nitqarun:** *"At the blessedly ripe moment is everyone who allows themselves to be living, perennial planters of peace, channels of Reality's creation moment. By hollowing themselves out (as the stalk of a plant allows nutrients to flow), they shall be engraved with the sign of Alaha, Reality itself."* (15)

Practical steps allow me to see previously unimagined possibilities that can come into form and to feel a new sense of my soul becoming fully embodied.

8. **Tubwayhun layleyn detrdep metol khenuta dilhounhie malkuta dashmaya:** *"Tuning to ripeness are those pushed consciously through the boundaries temporarily set by others or themselves, for the sake of inner honesty and outer justice. They are entering the larger life shining around them and being renewed by its vision and power."* (35)

I feel the caravan of ancestors—especially the teachers, prophets, healers, and artists who have inspired me—moving ahead of me. I consciously join them, strengthening my feeling of connection to the heart of those walking ahead of me. I affirm I will leave a legacy of inspiration for those traveling after me in the future.

9. **Tubwayhun immath damhasdeen l'khon waradpin l'khon wamrin elaykon kul milla bisha metolath b'dagalutha:** *Ripening now are those who, in the moment of being envied, pushed beyond their boundaries, spoken about unripely, follow my way and realize that all*

this is just the self's sticky web of pretense. (29. For this one, the book follows the similar passage in Luke 6:22 rather than Matthew 5:11. See RAJ for more on this.)

I screen out the negative messages, receive the gift of pure energy and attention behind them, and use these to travel further.

10. **Haydeyn hadaw wa rwazw d'agarkhun sgiy bashmaya hakhana geyr r'dapw l'nabiya d'men q'damaykhun:** *From the point of now, feel joy and guidance, the abundance of "what's just enough." Become the leading shoot of a new plant of Reality's growth spreading to connect the life of your soul with the power within all the souls traveling the prophetic caravan in front of and behind you.* (32)

My actual home is the cosmos. In the communion with nature, I find the one creation uniting me with all beings: my heart held within the heart of the Only Being, *Alaha.*

This retreat is best done over nine or ten days, with the final day spent integrating the wordless *shem* of the whole journey and gazing through the heart toward what life is presenting you in the time ahead.

SELECTED BIBLIOGRAPHY

For a full bibliography, see *Revelations of the Aramaic Jesus* (2022). Charlottesville: Hampton Roads.

A Biblical Aramaic Lexicon of the Old Testament (Abridged). (1999). Electronic text hypertexted and prepared by Accordance Bible Software, Oaktree Software, FL.

Greek New Testament (Nestle-Aland, 27th edition, second printing) (1995). Stuttgart: Deutsche Bibelgesellschaft. And via Accordance Software as above. (1993).

Syriac New Testament Peshitta (morphologically tagged). George A. Kiraz. Accordance Software. (1993).

Syriac-English New Testament: The Traditional Peshitta Text and the Antioch Bible English Translation. (2020). George A. Kiraz, ed. Piscataway: Gorgias Press.

Barfield, Owen. (1998). *Saving the Appearances: A Study in Idolatry*. Oxford: Barfield Press.

D'Olivet, Fabre. (1815). *The Hebraic Tongue Restored*. Nayan Louise Redfield, trans. 1921 edition republished 1991. York Beach, ME: Samuel Weiser.

Douglas-Klotz, Neil. (1999). *The Hidden Gospel: Decoding the Spirituality of the Aramaic Jesus*. Wheaton, IL: Quest Books.

Douglas-Klotz, Neil. (2011). *Desert Wisdom: A Nomad's Guide to Life's Big Questions from the Heart of the Native Middle East*. Edinburgh, Columbus: ARC Books.

Grondin, Michael W. (1998). *Interlinear Coptic/English Translation of the Gospel of Thomas and Coptic/English Lexicon*. Online at the Gnostic Society Library www.gnosis.org.

Kiraz, George Anton. (2002). *Comparative Edition of the Syriac Gospels: Aligning the Sinaiticus, Curetonianus, Peshitta and Harklean Versions*. Piscataway: Gorgias Press.

Sokoloff, Michael. (2009). *A Syriac Lexicon*. Piscataway: Gorgias Press.

Smith, J. Payne, ed. (1903). *A Compendious Syriac Dictionary*. Oxford: Clarendon Press.

Thomas, Robert L., ed. (1981). *New American Standard Exhaustive Concordance of the Bible: Hebrew-Aramaic Dictionary*. Electronic Edition. Vancouver, WA: Accordance Software.

SCRIPTURE INDEX

Luke 11:4   *page 85*

"And forgive us our sins; for we also forgive every one that is indebted to us."

Mark 3:28–29   *page 60*

"Verily I say unto you, all sins shall be forgiven unto the sons of men, and blasphemies wherewith soever they shall blaspheme. But he that shall blaspheme against the Holy Ghost hath never forgiveness but is in danger of eternal damnation."

Matt. 5:3, KJV translation   *page 12*

"Blessed are the poor in spirit, for theirs is the kingdom of heaven."

Matt. 5:4   *page 69*

"Blessed *are* they that mourn: for they shall be comforted."

Matt. 5:5   *page 75*

"Blessed are the meek: for they shall inherit the earth."

Matt. 5:6   *page 42*

"Blessed are they which do hunger and thirst after righteousness: for they shall be filled."

Matt. 5:7   *page 45*

"Blessed are the merciful: for they shall obtain mercy."

Matt. 5:8   *page 48*

"Blessed are the pure in heart: for they shall see God."

Matt. 5:9   *page 52*

"Blessed are the peacemakers: for they shall be called the children of God."

Matt. 5:10   *page 111*

"Blessed are they which are persecuted for righteousness' sake: for theirs is the kingdom of heaven."

Matt. 5:12   *page 103*

"Rejoice, and be exceeding glad: for great *is* your reward in heaven: for so persecuted they the prophets which were before you."

Matt. 5:14   *page 105*

"Ye are the light of the world. A city that is set on a hill cannot be hid."

Matt. 6:34　*page 121*

"Take therefore no thought for the morrow: for the morrow shall take thought for the things of itself. Sufficient unto the day is the evil thereof."

Matt. 7:7　*page 82*

"Ask, and it shall be given you; seek and ye shall find; knock, and it shall be opened unto you."

Matt. 9:17　*page 63*

"Neither do men put new wine into old bottles: else the bottles break, and the wine runneth out, and the bottles perish: but they put new wine into new bottles, and both are preserved." Also Mark 2:22, Luke 5:37.

Matt. 10:16　*page 124*

"Be ye therefore wise as serpents, and harmless as doves."

Matt. 10:39　*page 90*

"He that findeth his life shall lose it: and he that loseth his life for my sake shall find it."

Matt. 11:28　*page 67*

"Come unto me all ye that labour and are heavy laden, and I will give you rest. . . . For my yoke is easy and my burden is light."

Matt. 15:11, 17, 18　*page 18*

"Not that which goeth into the mouth defileth a man, but that which cometh out of the mouth, this defileth a man. Whatever entereth in at the mouth goeth into the belly, and is cast out into the draught. But those things which proceed out of the mouth come forth from the heart; and they defile the man."

Matt. 18:5　*page 54*

"Whoso shall receive one such little child in my name receiveth me."

Matt. 18:18　*page 73*

"Whatsoever ye shall bind on earth shall be bound in heaven: and whatsoever ye shall loose on earth shall be loosed in heaven."

Thomas 39　*page 33*

"The Pharisees and the scholars have taken the keys of knowledge and have hidden them. They have not entered, nor have they allowed those who want to enter to do so."

INDEX

MY BACKGROUND

From the Introduction to
Revelations of the Aramaic Jesus

My own parents were freethinking Christians, deeply involved in holistic health, organic gardening, and receiving wisdom from within. I like to say that, beyond being read Bible stories each night before bed, I was raised with a "holy trinity" of three C's: chiropractic, (Rachel) Carson, and (Edgar) Cayce. As part of Lutheran schooling, I also memorized large parts of the King James Bible translation as well as most of Luther's Small Catechism. While all this made for an unusual childhood, I never regretted it, yet I never would have anticipated becoming involved in Jesus's Aramaic language. It was only because I was also raised hearing multiple languages in the homes of my grandparents (German, Polish, Yiddish), that I thought, "how hard can it be?" Little did I know.

For several hundred years, the scholarly world has divided language, psychology, philosophy, spirituality, and science; so to make a long story short, my doctorate in religious studies ended up combining ancient Semitic language hermeneutics (interpretation theory) and somatic (body-oriented) psychology in order to be able to begin to articulate an epistemology (a way of knowing) that approached that of Yeshua. One also has to learn to use yet another language—the academic one. Yet my interest and passion were driven by childhood spiritual experiences of Jesus as well as later ones when I began to chant the first word of his prayer in Aramaic: *Abwun*. The academic study then became all about making connections that others largely had not, given the gifts I was born with and the tools I acquired.

Uniting both those who doubt whether Jesus said anything and those who believe he said everything that the Gospels report, the simple undeniable message of this book, as in my others, is that *when or if Jesus said anything, he said it in Aramaic.* Given this, why not look at his words and actions through the way of knowing built into his language?

NOTES/REFLECTIONS

ABOUT THE AUTHOR

Neil Douglas-Klotz, Ph.D., is a renowned writer in the fields of Middle Eastern spirituality and the translation and interpretation of the ancient Semitic languages of Hebrew, Aramaic, and Arabic. Living in Scotland, he was for many years co-chair of the Mysticism Group of the American Academy of Religion. A frequent speaker and workshop leader, he is the author of several books. His books on the Aramaic spirituality of Jesus include *Revelations of the Aramaic Jesus, Prayers of the Cosmos, The Hidden Gospel, Original Meditation,* and *Blessings of the Cosmos.* His books on a comparative view of Native Middle Eastern spirituality include *Desert Wisdom: A Nomad's Guide to Life's Big Questions* and *The Tent of Abraham* (with Rabbi Arthur Waskow and Sr. Joan Chittister). His books on Sufi spirituality include *The Sufi Book of Life: 99 Pathways of the Heart for the Modern Dervish* and *A Little Book of Sufi Stories.* His biographical collections of the works of his Sufi teachers include *Sufi Vision and Initiation* (Samuel L. Lewis) and *Illuminating the Shadow* (Moineddin Jablonski). He has also written a mystery novel set in the first century CE Holy Land entitled *A Murder at Armageddon.*

In addition, he recently edited five "Little Books" published by Hampton Roads, four devoted to a new selection of the work of Lebanese American writer, poet, and mystic Kahlil Gibran, and one dedicated to *Wild Wisdom,* a collection of early ecological writers and mystics.

For more information about his work, see the website of the Abwoon Network (*https://abwoon.org*) or visit his Facebook page (*www.facebook.com/AuthorNeilDouglasKlotz/*)

TO OUR READERS

HAMPTON ROADS PUBLISHING, an imprint of Red Wheel/Weiser, publishes inspirational books from a variety of spiritual traditions and philosophical perspectives for "the evolving human spirit."

Our readers are our most important resource, and we appreciate your input, suggestions, and ideas about what you would like to see published.

Visit our website at *www.redwheelweiser.com*, where you can learn about our upcoming books and also find links to sign up for our newsletter and exclusive offers.

You can also contact us at *info@rwwbooks.com* or at

Red Wheel/Weiser, LLC
65 Parker Street, Suite 7
Newburyport, MA 01950